WITHDRAWN

JOURNEY THROUGH DREAD

A study of Kierkegaard, Heidegger
and Sartre.

Soeren Kierkegaard

Journey
Through Dread

A study of Kierkegaard, Heidegger
and Sartre.

by

ARLAND USSHER

BIBLO and TANNEN
NEW YORK
1968

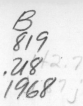

Copyright 1955 by Arland Ussher

Reprinted, 1968, by

Biblo and Tannen Booksellers and Publishers, Inc.
63 Fourth Avenue   New York, N.Y. 10003

This book has been reprinted by special permission
of the original publishers, Devin-Adair Company,
23 East 26th Street, New York, N. Y. 10010.

Permission to reprint material from this book must
be obtained in writing from them.

Library of Congress Catalog Card No. 68-54234

Printed in U.S.A. by
NOBLE OFFSET PRINTERS, INC.
NEW YORK 3, N. Y.

CONTENTS

ACKNOWLEDGEMENTS

I should like to thank the Princeton University Press and the American-Scandinavian Foundation for permission to quote passages from Kierkegaard's *Either/Or, Philosophical Fragments* and *Concluding Unscientific Postscript*.

LIST OF ILLUSTRATIONS

The explanation of the irrational is the special task of the twentieth century.—M. MERLEAU-PONTY.

The Son of God was crucified; I am unashamed of it because men must needs be ashamed of it. And the Son of God died; it is by all means to be believed, because it is absurd. And He was buried and rose again; the fact is certain because it is impossible.—TERTULLIAN, *De Carne Christi*.

If, then, the things which differ from God, and from which God differs, lose what existence they had whilst they are undergoing change, wherein will consist the difference of the. Divine Being from all other things except in His possessing the contrary faculty· to theirs—in other words, that God can be changed into all conditions, and yet continue just as He is?—TERTULLIAN, *De Carne Christi*.

INTRODUCTION

SYNOPSIS

Existentialism is a philosophy for thought-adventurers, as our title implies—a way of thinking for an age of experiment, tension and stress. This book is not concerned with all the varieties of Existentialism, but specifically with the " philosophy of dread "—with three thinkers who have often been decried, and partly misunderstood, on account of their " pessimism ". That pessimism is not of the passive Schopenhauerian kind, but is rather a bracing sense of the menace and challenge of existence. Existentialism is dramatic, often melodramatic—like the Hegelianism from which it so largely sprang, it may tend towards egocentricity. On the other hand, it has the virtue of avoiding a complacent, anæmic, rationalism. It is not a philosophy " for all time ", but it may be appropriate and serviceable for a time of transition—and even for all time in so far as all times are transitional. It cannot give us a complete system, because it sees every human situation as incomplete. It calls on us to choose, but it cannot propose objects for our choice, because no two situations are the same; the Existentialist must " travel light " and pick up his categories, or drop them, as he goes. Here we seem to get a hint of an older, perhaps more gracious philosophy—the " Wandering in the Great Void " of the Buddhist and Taoist: the " Existential Will ", when it learns to know itself and trust itself, may make men well adjusted, and therefore free.

IT is no fault of mine if the title of this book suggests a " thriller ". " Philosophy in the manner of a thriller " is one famous definition of Existentialism.[1] Existential philosophy arose alongside the modern novel, and much of

[1] Guido de Ruggiero, *Existentialism*.

9

what is good and not-so-good in it is attributable to its novelistic technique. Existentialism sees life as an adventure rather than a scheme—a play in which we pick up our parts as we go along; and it is therefore appropriate to an age in which the moulds of life and thought are broken. Or, as we may put it in the more romantic terms of Jaspers, it is a " philosophy of night "—a way of thought for a time in which men must walk alone, groping their way, and when all distances and proportions dissolve in relativity. In a word, with Existentialism—at least in its later phases—we are in the climate of Einstein, Picasso and Freud.

This book makes no attempt to deal with the whole Existentialist movement. To do so, it would have to take in philosophers so far apart as the Spaniard Ortega y Gasset, the American Reinhold Niebuhr and the Russian Nicolai Berdyaev. It would have to speak of the Protestant renascence associated with Karl Barth and Emil Brunner, and also of the Judaist Chassidic contribution—which finds such noble expression in Martin Buber. It would need, above all, to include some study of Gabriel Marcel and Karl Jaspers: both of them important thinkers, and the real founders of Existentialism in their respective countries. It would need to bestow more than a glance on such forerunners as Pascal and de Biran, Hamann, Jacobi and, of course, Nietzsche. My aim is a more modest one. This book is an account of three men whom I myself happen to have found challenging and moving—two of whom I believe to be undervalued in England, where their type of thought is very repugnant to the national temper. It relates a personal voyage of discovery, and I cannot help it if the viewpoints are very personal also. When therefore I speak of Existentialism, I must be understood to refer specifically to the philosophy of *Dread*—in all senses of that word, ranging from the holy awe of Kierkegaard to the more mundane shudders of Sartre. There is almost nothing of this in Marcel; and even Jaspers conveys little of it, though he describes the supreme experience as "shipwreck" (*Scheitern*), which sounds sufficiently formidable. On the other hand, I shall have to speak much of Hegel, whose thought-forms underlie the whole movement as those of Aristotle underlay Scholasticism; and who, with his dynamic *Sturm und Drang*, may be called the invisible master of the revels.

The Existentialism I write of corresponds to a certain way of looking at the world, prevalent today but common of course in all times, and not least among quite unintellectual persons. It stresses a few very simple and fundamental emotions—the unreasoned sense of guilt (Kierkegaard), the mingled fear and nostalgia in the anticipation of death (Heidegger), the feeling, deriving from it, of perpetual challenge (Sartre). Freudians have their own names for these things, but I do not consider them unhealthy in themselves, even if my three subjects (like many other men of great genius) seem often to verge upon morbidity. Existentialism is not necessarily either the pessimism of a Schopenhauer or the optimism of a Hegel, but varies from the feelings of a prisoner on the night before his execution to the sheer zest experienced in living, and thinking, dangerously. It is obvious that it is a dangerous philosophy: taken " neat ", it can end in something like the " gratuitous crime " of Gide—the state of mind of the man who throws a bomb, or of the child who commits an indecency, just to see what will happen, or to show that he is not afraid. There is much of this feeling in Sartre, together with genuine libertarian emotion and a Shavian scorn of the " humbugs " (which is the nearest polite rendering of *les salauds*). Sartre, like Rousseau, is that most embarrassing of all spectacles to the " humbugs "—a man of fine intellect and generous temper, but (as he is not ashamed to let us feel) with many of the instincts of a *voyou*.

This raises the question, which cannot be passed over,

whether Existentialism is radically evil in its nature; for the deification of the Will, like that of the Void, has always something Satanic. This will scarcely be urged in the case of Kierkegaard, who has inspired in some quarters almost a revival of primitive Christianity; nevertheless, Kierkegaard's doctrine of a " suspension of the Ethical " held the germ of all that is dubious in Existentialism today. Existentialism in fact is not uncontaminated by the Idealism (in the philosophic sense) against which it arose as a protest. As in Idealism the Self or Subject really exists in a Void, a masquerade of appearances, so in Existentialism the Void—comparable to the Djinn in the Arabian Nights' tale—has, so to say, been made flesh and become the Self. Both the two philosophies, apparently opposite, can easily be expanded into complete nihilism; for Nothingness is an idea whose nature it is to spread, like a drop of ink in blotting-paper, and the Void (whether conceived as within us or without) is the very notion of the all-indrawing Abyss. I do not think Heidegger really escapes that extreme—" the nightmare of German genius " as F. A. Voigt has called it. Existentialism lacks, however, what is the greatest vice of Idealism, at least in its later phases—I mean a cowardly complacency. Its very appearance of pessimism is its redeeming feature, for, as has been said, the scoundrels all are optimists. Existentialism starts where every religion starts, but where philosophy up till Kierkegaard had barely arrived: in an anguished awareness of Evil. Kierkegaard raised his voice against Hegel to protest that Sin is *not* mere Negation or " Mediation ". Sartre retorted to an easy æsthetic Idealism that, as we have sorrowfully learned, Evil *cannot* be redeemed.

This, like so many other important discussions, is largely a matter of emphasis. Hegel's intensely dramatic philosophy was not, like the eighteenth-century rationalism, meant to minimise the tragic; and even Flaubert did not pretend the *laideur* of existence is removed by being stylishly described!

On the other hand, if life can be represented at all in abstract terms (as all philosophies have hitherto held) then Evil *is* Negation; and if there is *some* universal balancing of things (as all religions have held) then it *is* redeemed—in the sense of compensated for. To say that " Evil cannot be redeemed " is either tautological or it is untrue. An English philosopher would be content to say more simply that Evil is a fact; unless, of course, he were too " practical " or " scientific " to recognise the fact. Nevertheless, philosophies of reason and order, of which Idealism is the type, tend to a callousness and a conceit of omniscience; and Existentialism's stress on the reality and *solidity* of Evil (and even simply of oppression or ugliness) makes it both timely and indeed refreshing. It does not, like Ivan Karamazov, " hand back the entrance-ticket " of existence, but like him it refuses to accept the world as a professor's faultless scheme.

It may be said that there are two alternative ways of approaching any new philosophy. The first is cautiously to welcome it, as likely to contain some novel truth, or an old truth adapted to new circumstance. (I would say " a part of the Truth ", but that some Socratic questioner would at once ask, " How can you tell that it is a part unless you have seen the whole? " To which the shortest answer is, " I might give a guess. I would guess that a camel's foot was a foot without having seen a camel ".) The second is to denounce it roundly, with some gracious concessions, for not being the whole and sole Truth—which, it is assumed, has in essentials once for all been given. The latter is, quite logically and consistently, the attitude of the doctors of Roman Catholic Thomism—and, without any logic, that of the partisans of almost every other school. Actually by far the best critiques of non-Catholic Existentialism, at least in the English-speaking world, have been written by Thomists. The first of the above positions, however, is the one I find most congenial, and which I mean to adopt; as I should likewise do in looking back to the (possibly superior, but to me rather remote and unserviceable) philosophy of Aquinas. But it must be kept in mind that this attitude has its own danger—the danger of mere modishness and novelty-hunting. Those persons who swallow Sartre whole (as in another generation they would have swallowed Bergson or Comte), simply because it is, or was yesterday, up to date to do so, are of course stupider than any obscurantist. There *is*, however, such a thing as the *Zeitgeist*—the changing response demanded by a changing set of problems. If Existentialists speak of the Abyss, the Leap, Crisis, Dread and whatnot, it is because these things are the realities of our present situation. Some time between the two wars, those Kantian skeletons the " Things-in-themselves " walked out of their closets; or in different words, the Nothing was made flesh and laid a cold hand on our hearts.

Existentialism is certainly no complete or final philosophy. It is not even a single philosophy; and Heidegger has repudiated even the name! Implicitly, indeed, it denies that anything human can be complete or final. For Sartre every value, or order of values, is the creation of a particular man in a particular situation, true and valid only for him. And words being what they are—fallible tools invented by imperfect beings for limited practical ends—one may well doubt the finality of all verbal constructions. Marxists call Existentialism the Last Phase of Bourgeois Capitalism—it is surprising how many things have been called the Last Phase of Capitalism! But in fact it is the last phase of something rather more important than capitalism: namely the Western belief in words, concepts and objectified values. Its language is evocative and often incantatory, and in so far as this is unadmitted it is dangerous. But even in attacking categories and concepts, Existentialism is naturally forced to make use of them; largely, as I have said, it employs the conceptual forms of Hegel, though with a psychological reference rather than a logical one. Apart from this, however, it is clear that Existentialism does not fit human existence at its lighter and happier moments. There are few roses among its thorns. It is anti-traditional; it is urban and does not take Nature naturally, in spite of some lyric pæans from Kierkegaard and Heidegger. It calls the non-logical the " absurd ", but gives the word an unduly sombre and austere signification (corresponding, in Sartre, to a contemporary mood, for which unfortunately there is only too much reason). It is indeed the Ugly Duckling among philosophies —but one which, because it feels itself to be such, *may* grow into a swan.

To me, at least, there is hope in its insistence, perverse or anarchic as it may be, on the individual; for that is where we start from. Faith, hope and charity (apart from the customary motions) may be left till later; otherwise we shall only get our faith from the Church, our hope from the Press, and our charity from the Welfare State. The individual today has come to " Years of Indiscretion ", and *been given his latchkey*; but he is frightened, and only too anxious to surrender it again. He finds himself " thrown " into an unfriendly world, and confronted with a Demon—his own naked Will. Its symbol is the discovery of machine-power, which has made us, to our dismay, " as gods ". We have lost all our Edens—even the socialist one in the future; our very continuance as a race depends, no longer merely on instincts we share with the animals, but on our Will. In the primitive human being, the Will was attached to Instinct, as if held by a father's hand; in the Western Man of history, it was subjected to a norm of Reason, like a boy's copy-book. But today Instinct has failed, and school-book rules seem inadequate to the complexity of life: the modern man finds himself before a chasm—his own Will. He can leap it only by *choosing*—creating for himself a Self, an Essence. There is no evading the necessity, for if he refuse to choose, that also is a negative choice. Naturally he had better choose "right", but to propound bare ideals or principles is really muddle-headed: it is attempting to bring him back to the *Instinct* of the nursery or the mere *Reason* of the school. Even if he is religious, he will reserve freedom of "interpretation"; even if he is a rationalist, he will argue from his own premisses. Granted that the Will should be the Good Will, what do we mean by the Good? Who is to say what will make men happy? Was Cromwell right? Or Lincoln? Or Lenin? Who will dare to say? Should I be writing this book, or distributing baked beans to refugee children? Am I justified in serving my country in an unjust war? Should I rescue first my mother or my sweetheart if both have fallen in the water? Does virtue or vice make the better poet? And is poetry better or not better than virtue?[1] Only fools or blackguards will venture to be dogmatic. In all important decisions one must choose one's order of values—even if it should mean, as boys say, " Choose and be damned ".

That is Existentialism's last word; but perhaps there is another word to be said. According to the old wisdom of the East, man suffers because he is at odds, not with Heaven, but with Nature (the *Tao*): not with the " Idea ", but with the Real. Abstract reason cannot give him the right adjustment, but artistic intuition—a sort of physical tact—perhaps can. He can be as " free " as a bird on the wing, in an immediate rhythmic unity with the environment that supports him[2]:

[1] It is a sign of how little accustomed most people are to " Existential " thinking, that these puzzles are still endlessly argued. Yet clearly there can be no answers to them capable of general application. (This was Kierkegaard's meaning, which he obscured by his Biblical examples and by that unfortunate phrase, a " suspension of the ethical ". It is also an entirely rational explanation of the human feeling—concerning which Jaspers has written well—of inescapable *guilt*.) The attempt to found a science of casuistry was made once for all by the Jesuits. The endeavour was honest, but it led to ludicrous results, which involved the Order in discredit.

[2] Compare Sartre's excellent symbol of the ski-er in *L'Etre et le Néant*.

but only if he has sense of the precariousness, indeed the horror, of his situation. To " hold on " to a thing, to hold on to a truth or value, is to lose it[1]—for the stream will not be grasped and held; wisdom begins where morality and system end. The highest human being is he who makes of himself a " Nothing ", a mere *openness* to the world. Reason separates man from man—four centuries of rationalism have only drawn the Westerner closer to the vortex of solipsism— love and idealistic dreaming make him mad; but the dumb sense of the right *occasion* can unite. Knowledge is not to be found in the strife of tongues, but in the " Great Void "; spirits (" essences ") inhabit, not men, but stones; life is short and death-shadowed, but men's wandering and wondering are long. Is not this near to the doctrines of the Existentialists—but with a different accent, a more engaging air? Could it not lead eventually to new cultivation (vital to our economics as to our art) of the local, the intimate, the personal: even to forgotten things like manners and style? The way—from where we are—may be a long one, but I see a tiny gleam of hope in the Existential will.

---

[1] Compare with this the aphorism of the Existentialist Leo Chestov, " One cannot say of God that he exists, for in saying ' God exists ' one loses him immediately ". Or Karl Barth's somewhat equivocal pronouncement, " God is a subject and not an object "; or even the (rather surprising) remark of Gabriel Marcel, " Je ne sais pas ce que je crois ".

I

SYNOPSIS: KIERKEGAARD

Kierkegaard began by loving despair, and ended by rationalising it as belief in the impossible. He is great because of the tragic tension of Will implied in this attempt. And yet, living among myths, he seems himself more a myth than a man. He waited for an event which, because he could only wait for it, did not happen; and he could imagine the motion of the spirit merely in terms of faery magic, a divine-dæmonic possession. But again, the suffering involved in such failure seemed to him the proof of his success. In willing suffering, and in studying his suffering self objectively, he realised himself as Subjectivity and as Will. Kierkegaard's mistake lay in condemning the Æsthetic, which alone can unite the subject with the object. In this sense, he contrasted the " genius " (such as Socrates was) with the Christian apostle, and saw the former as a mere ironist. Having such a conception of art and philosophy, he remained, as philosopher and artist, no more than an ironist himself. Kierkegaard became indeed a mystic—but one who knew, of mysticism, only the solitude and dread. But it is for this that he appeals to the sceptical modern man, who is making discovery of himself through solitude and through dread.

Kierkegaard cannot be understood unless we understand and do justice to Hegel; for Kierkegaard, like Marx (though in a different sense), merely inverted Hegelianism. Hegel was (in essence) a religious romantic, for whom all discord was " harmony not understood ", and who believed he had found the key to make it understandable. That key was the Dialectic, which seemed to unlock every door—except (as Kierkegaard pointed out) the Future; for it could not serve as a guide to action. The Dialectic represented, in fact, the final defeat of philosophy; for concrete particulars will evade even the best-conceived abstract pattern. Kierkegaard felt that any such preordained pattern was the negation of willing, suffering man. He saw the Dialectic as a glorified amateurism, a cosmic playing-with-masks. The Hegelian philosopher had to wait for other men to act before he could philosophise about it. Such a vision as Hegel's might be true for a contemplator at the end of time—not for an actor involved in the time-process. Moreover in idealising the actual, Hegel left no room for dreams and aspirations. Whatever chanced to happen was commanded by " historic logic ". Hegel, however, believed he was interpreting Christianity, which points to the Incarnation as the actualisation of Godhead. The world, for him, was—by extension—the passion of Man. Thus Kierkegaard's stress on the pathetic was a mere application to practice of what Hegel had shown in a paradigm. With Kierkegaard, the tragedian Man throws off the " unities " of the Hegelian world-drama.

If Hegel's concepts were ghosts, it may equally be said that Kierkegaard lived among ghosts; but he lived among them so intensely that he brought them to life.

I

KIERKEGAARD

THE SHUDDER BEFORE GOD

There he stands, the ambassador from the kingdom of sighs, the chosen favourite of the realm of suffering, the apostle of grief, the silent friend of pain, the unhappy lover of memory, in his memories confounded by the light of hope, in his hope deceived by the shadows of memory. . . . I hail thee with thy title of honour, the Unhappiest Man! . . . Accept then our wish, a good wish: May no one understand you, may all men envy you; may no friend bind himself to you, may no woman love you; may no secret sympathy suspect your lonely pain, may no eye pierce your distant grief; may no ear trace your secret sigh![1]

THESE lines, by the young Kierkegaard, are revealing —even though (as so often in his early works) he is not here speaking in his own person. It was in a quite different sense that, in the same work, he counselled us to " choose despair ". We were to choose despair in order, through that very encounter, to be freed from its power— despair which, he held, was always latent and near the surface in " æsthetic " or epicurean living. But it is easier to leap into despair than to leap out of it. It may be disputed whether Kierkegaard ever in fact passed beyond despair, or whether he merely sounded, with a sort of perverse hopefulness, every crevice and cranny of that condition. Because he was a great soul, he aimed at, and almost attained, the impossible—the impossible aim of " believing the impossible "; and he has turned the thought of a later generation

[1] *Either/Or*: I. " *The Unhappiest Man.*"

21

back to inwardness. As Wilde said of Hamlet (in so many ways his prototype), " The world has become sad because a puppet was once melancholy ". But it will always be a question whether he really sought sainthood through despair, or whether he was fascinated by despair when he thought he was in love with sainthood.

Kierkegaard was a true Existentialist in this sense, that—herein like Nietzsche—his life interests us almost more than his doctrines: only that his doctrines, unlike those of Nietzsche, were intimately related to his life (a relationship which, of course, is fundamental to Existentialism). If his was a " split " character, he was to this extent at least harmonious; there was about him none of that rather comic incongruity which is the final impression left on us by the creator of Zarathustra. Nietzsche dreamed of war, wine and song while leading the existence of a timid recluse; Kierkegaard both advocated inwardness and lived it. Yet he was always a great observer, mingling with delight in the life of the streets, and, like so different a man as Sartre, was a great " man of the cafés ". He said that he should have been a spy, and there was confessedly something a little equivocal and " underground " in his nature; it is part of the eternal problem of how far he remained to the end a romantic actor. But in reading his life we are almost in the atmosphere of *Wuthering Heights*, and Hogg's *Memoirs of a Justified Sinner*, and George Borrow's tale of the Welsh pastor—the man who thought he had committed the Unpardonable Sin.

And yet this man, who gives so intense and even terrifying an impression of reality, to all appearance scarcely lived at all! At first view, he would seem, again like Nietzsche, to have been a contradiction. His writings, with all their wit, their depth, and *at times* their moving sorrow, have a curious lack of solidity. They show us someone praising existence, will and decision who passed through life a little like a ghost: who was as ignorant of his time and (except externally) of

22

other human beings as the professors whom he mocked; who was apparently unable to imagine a world in which religious postulates were not accepted: who, while he talked of relating oneself to the future, lived like Quixote in an age which had passed. Or one might compare him to his early hero, the Wandering Jew Ahasuerus—passing unheeding through world events which hardly touched him, in expectation of a Second Coming which never came. The elder Kierkegaard, who in anguished childhood had cursed God— the father who kept the young Soeren entranced with imaginary promenades, encounters and disputations—that legend-like figure had predestined his son to a double role: the double role of a penitent and a player. Kierkegaard passed from the " æsthetic " phase to the " religious " phase—but he really missed the " ethical " (that is to say the social, extravert) phase, which according to his theory should have lain between them.[1] Which is another way of saying that he never wholly came out of the " æsthetic " phase. Reared (like J. H. Newman) on myths, he was to dream all his life of a *true* Myth—the fairy tale which philosophy could not philosophise nor poetry poeticise away: and to the support of this " Paradox " he was to summon all his amazing philosophic and poetic resources. But the Myth remained a myth for him—he could never marry Time and Eternity, Hegel and Luther—dreaming of Heaven he lived, like his father or Ahasuerus, under Heaven's curse.

Fairy tales abound in the earlier and gentler Kierkegaard, though already the problems in these parables place a heavy

[1] The " æsthetic " and the " religious ", according to Kierkegaard, are both phases of concealment; in the first a man relates himself to himself, in the second to God. Little, however, is said of relations with *others*—lacking which the Self must remain slightly dwarfish and infantile, while God is merely distant and awe-inspiring. For Kierkegaard, as for his German teachers (though with an opposite implication to theirs), the ethical life meant the wholly public and external life.

burden on the poetry. And of course they were always the same problem—and the same story. In one of the many variants of this story, a merman who seduces a mortal maid is vexed with a dilemma; though wishing to wed the girl, he finds he cannot do so—for marriage is the " ethical ", and he who has once sinned can never return to the ethical phase, but must pass his life as a penitent. This seems to restrict the ethical to small compass indeed! But in fact Kierkegaard could not imagine sorrow or humility as anything less than *despair*—a soul-shattering crisis. The ethical person for him (against whom he understandably revolts) is the bourgeois Protestant of Fichtean or Hegelian German moralism, conditioned to a clock-like performance of duty, and to whom repentance is a reprehensible waste of time. Therefore when at last, quitting verisimilitude, his merman marries the maiden, he cannot be behaving ethically (for repentance is " beyond ethics ") but is saved, like Faust, by a miracle—described in the usual tortuous phraseology. " Having performed the infinite movement of repentance, he performs still one more movement, the movement by virtue of the absurd." How Kierkegaard imagined this manœuvre —in the story as in his life—remains very obscure; because in his life, as we know, the miracle failed to happen. Love for Kierkegaard was always, for good and for ill, a ravishment (which is the real meaning of the " leap "): the act in which the marine demon seizes the maiden, or the Divine possesses the passive contrite soul. The first he called the æsthetic, the second the religious; and between them the ethical got lost. Unfitted by nature for the active role, Kierkegaard threw himself ardently into the passive one. Atoning for the " demon " he envied and could never be, he ended by making God Himself the Demon.

I have said that Kierkegaard never really got away from æstheticism—as, it is admitted, he never wrenched himself free of Hegel. The judgment may seem unjust, seeing that he believed for a time (with startling literalness) in the faith that can move mountains. But it was the belief in faery magic of a countryman of Hans Andersen: it was not, as he came to realise, true faith. He had convinced himself that God would somehow restore to him the fiancée he had given up, as He restored to Abraham his Isaac and to Job his oxen[1], being satisfied with the anguish He had imposed on him and on her as a mere test; but Kierkegaard knew in the end that, by making a gratuitous sacrifice, he had himself been trying to test God. " If I had had faith," he was to say, " I would have stayed with Regine." Like Moses he had struck the rock—like the first Christians he had expected a new heaven and a new earth: this Faust had called on Jesus to work the wizardry of Mephistopheles, and the Hegelian magic had not worked for him. He knew it in fact when Regine, little versed in the twists of a mystical dialectic, consoled herself in a bourgeois marriage. It is of course true that later in life Kierkegaard extolled asceticism, and called on Protestants to bring back the monastery; given his religious premises, he was right. Evangelical Protestantism combines, illogically, a more-than-monkish denunciation of the world and the flesh with the example of a married—and very mundane— ministry. Kierkegaard's earlier notion of the " Knight of Faith " who outwardly might be any tax inspector (like the Arjuna of the Bhagavad Gita who is told to fight and kill, though without enthusiasm) was a romantic fallacy. But Kierkegaard, one feels certain, could never have been a monk; he was as near to the truth, essentially, when he

---

[1] Kierkegaard seems to have believed, at the time of his discovery of the father's " guilt ", that God had given the latter wordly riches only the more effectively to destroy him. But this notion is surely Greek rather than Protestant or even Christian. In his fable *Solomon's Dream* he sees in King David's glories a mark of the divine wrath—a notion for which there is no warrant in the Old Testament. Nor does it accord with his doctrine of " Repetition ", as outlined in the book of that name and in *Fear and Trembling*.

broke with Regine on the pretence that he was a libertine.[1]

Kierkegaard was a great Lutheran, in a world in which the strange theology of Lutheranism had died as an effective creed. Which means that he was a Quixote of religion[2]— and it will never be decided whether Quixote was an enthusiast or (in part) a self-dramatiser. In this he differs from the great Jansenist who is so often compared with him, Pascal, whose temperament was that of the mathematician rather than the poet. As Kierkegaard, when a small boy, had walked and talked with his father in their gloomy house, out of which he " almost never went "—and merely imagined the other persons—so he was to walk and talk all his life with the heavenly Father, in a world of shadows.[3] As he had been the father's Benjamin, so he was (though with trembling) the elect child of God. (God the Son remained always more distant: He was the " Sign of Contradiction " merely, the Dialectical Negation, the " Offence " sent to test—and therefore by Hegelian logic to call forth—our faith.[4]) But how is the Vessel of Election

[1] " I could almost believe, to explain the contradictions which wrestle in me, that I am an Irishman. That people cannot bear to plunge their children completely in the baptismal water. They leave the right arm free, so that it may carry the sword or encircle a girl's waist."–*Journals*.

[2] It seems entirely appropriate that the Spanish poet-thinker Miguel Unamuno should have derived from Kierkegaard a philosophy of Quixotism.

[3] " I have, quite literally, lived with God as one lives with one's father."—*Journals*.

[4] Kierkegaard defines faith as a passionate inward appropriation of the objectively uncertain—even (he implies) the objectively improbable. Such " intuition ", though apparently absurd or verbally paradoxical, can be, in itself, both penetrating and profound; Tertullian's desperate, *Certum est quia impossibile* remains a fine saying. Kierkegaard, however was a great reasoner, and like all will-philosophers was forever " rationalising " his certainty with dubious logic (and such questionable definitions as the one above-quoted). Take for instance the following: " If He really were the Son of God, the proof would be ridiculous, just as ridiculous as though a man were to prove his own existence, since in this case Christ's existence and His divinity are the same ".—*Journals*. This

to be sure that he is indeed a Vessel of Election, and not of Destruction? How is he to know that his choices are activated by Divine Grace? How can he feel any certainty, above all, seeing that the Knight of Faith must live disguised even from himself? For a Kierkegaard there can be but one answer—the answer which has always been implicit in Protestantism and Jansenism: he can be assured only by the fact that he is extremely unhappy about it![1] Only in *willing suffering* can he feel that he is, like the God-Man Himself, an exception and a contradiction to the natural order: in Kierkegaard's terms, living paradoxically. Only by experiencing the maximum of misery can he feel the maximum of certainty—or rather, I should have said, a minimum of certainty, for of course this test also might be a ruse of the Devil[2], and *complete* certainty might cancel the misery. Only by being a sacrificial Isaac would he recognise himself for the beloved of Abraham: and no miracle (he knew in the end) would intervene. Kierkegaard, braver or more logical than Luther himself, did not shrink from the conclusion. It would be hard to say whether he left Regine because he felt called to follow God, or whether he was convinced of his calling

is like saying, " I cannot prove that I am Mr Smith, because I and Mr. Smith are the same ". I do not know what our immigration officers would think of such an argument.

[1] " Anxiety and dread constitute the only conceivable justification which can be thought. . . ."—*Fear and Trembling*.

[2] " Silence is the snare of the demon; and the more one keeps silent the more terrible the demon becomes; but silence is also the state in which the Individual becomes conscious of his union with the divinity." —*Fear and Trembling*. Kierkegaard, one may observe, refrains from mentioning His Satanic Majesty; and it is to his credit that, even in his sermons, he speaks nowhere of Hell-Fire. Indeed Kierkegaard (strange as it may seem) was apparently not much interested in his " soul " or in the Other World; the philosophical idealists were the objects of his attack—almost never the materialists. It is as if the dramatic " dialectical " adventure of faith were all he cared about. Hence it has been easy for his descendants, Heidegger and Sartre, to strip off the Christian husk from the voluntarist kernel.

27

through having left his sweetheart—because he had inflicted gratuitous suffering on himself and on her. We can imagine this Tertullian-in-love saying: " I leave her because it is absurd "—an inverted Don Juan, giving pain that he might receive it. Nor must we forget the Hegelian—the third component (however fiercely repudiated) in the make-up of this amazing man. In the dialectic he had taken or adapted from Hegel, the ethical was the negative phase, so that in turning his back on the ethical—in breaking (but with anguish) what he regarded as his plighted faith—he was behaving most ethically. He was both libertine and saint, and how else than by being a libertine for God could he " mediate the contraries "?[1]

There is an anecdote related by Kierkegaard in the *Journals* that the father had once remarked significantly (in reply to some " dangerous " sally from young Soeren) that " there are certain crimes which can only be striven against with God's help ". The boy, immediately he could slip away, ran to the mirror, to see whether he could detect in his features the signs of dawning criminality.[2] This story, which so well conveys the atmosphere of that guilt-haunted family,

[1] It has naturally been much discussed, in Kierkegaard's case as in Swift's, whether there was a physical disability. It is true that Kierkegaard has left us many mysterious hints which point to this conclusion; but then Kierkegaard loved mysteries. The stories of his visits to prostitutes in student days would not seem to accord with it; and neither does the fancy—which so often appears in his writings—of a man who had engendered in ignorance. On the other hand it is probable that, as with so many young men of puritanic or intraverted character, his guilt-feelings would have led to fiasco in a case of idealistic love. Also one may surmise what a Freudian has called his "sublimated incestuous homosexual relationship with his father ". If this jargon means that his feelings for his father prevented him ever really caring for anyone else, there is nothing extravagant in the notion; and it is surely the phrasing, and not the thought, which would have surprised Kierkegaard's contemporaries.

[2] One recalls the thrilling moment in a once popular romance: " Coming to my room, I saw for the first time the appearance of Edward Hyde."

is also suggestive in another sense. One feels that the young Soeren looked often in mirrors. For " reflective " natures, it always seems to me, the early view of the facial reflexion must be a telling experience. The other Self who is *not* there seems at the same time more uncanny and more intimately real than the mere other people who *are* there; and it is the mirror which, by turning the person back on himself, first sunders him from his kind. Somewhat in this manner, ever since the sixteenth century, when European man first commenced (so to speak) to study himself in the mirror—to regard himself objectively—he has been more and more concerned with the non-existent other Self, less and less with the existing other persons. Even the God of Protestants, as He became ever more of an intimate Presence, was decreasingly an independent (and accessible) Person. And the philosophies of the post-Reformation, whether " idealist " or " sensationalist ", have seen the world by analogy as the Mind's looking-glass, as a screen laid across Nothing. But there is of course (and this is the *second* discovery) a great difference between my mirror-image and the Other Person in the street outside: the image mysteriously follows my movements and my changes of expression—not so the Other Person. Looking in the mirror I become, as it were, a spirit hovering outside myself, watching myself; my monistic screen-world is finally torn in two. Paradoxically it is the mirror-image, the ironic double, which confutes the solipsist, by opening a window through his own infinity—a window upon himself! Thus the mirror, which at first cut me off from my fellows, ends by driving me inward upon my own subjectivity, the tangle of possibilities of which I am composed; in Kierkegaard's terms it turns me, at length, from an " æsthetic " or surface man to a " religious " one. The result is a profound disturbance, comparable to the mortal shock suffered by Wilde's hero when he slashed his picture. Like the baffled child who breaks his looking-glass, I am

Kierkegaard said, " can only be understood backward, but it must be lived forward." Like the ingenious, strangely unsensual, ironist of the *Seducer's Diary*, Socrates also was a " seducer of youth ", a player with interesting possibilities.[1] The Athenian lacked the sense of the *Instant*, as Greek statuary never achieved the *Look* (a remark which, as we shall see, brings Kierkegaard close to Sartre[2]. As Kierkegaard contrasted the Hegelian " mediation " (a logical process only) with the Mediatorship of Christ, so he opposed the Platonic " recollection " to a concept which he called " repetition "—by which he meant, at first, a recompense such as was made to Job (and to the repentant merman) and, later, the grateful acceptance of the lack of any such recompense. Plato, as is well known, held that truth is hidden in a man like a precious metal in a mine, to be brought to light by the shovel-work of dialectic: a notion which he connected with the myth of pre-existence, though we today may see in it an anticipation of the Unconscious. (It has, incidentally, an obvious closeness of feeling with his other famous myth—that of the Prisoners in the Cave.) Kierkegaard contrasts this with the soul's appropriation of religious truth. Socrates (the mere " genius ") compared himself to a midwife, bringing to birth fruits of the past; the Christian apostle, on the other hand, himself fertilises the soul of the believer, by transmission of the fecundating Word. Through the first I " repeat myself backwards," through the second I " remember myself forwards." I

[1] Nevertheless, the Socrates whom Kierkegaard admired was almost solely Socrates the ironist. Socrates' irony in regard to the contrast between his Exterior and his Essence (a contrast apparently in contradiction with the Hegelian theory of " coincidence ") was particularly pleasing to the hunchback, Kierkegaard. Kierkegaard might have noticed that it also contradicted, in appearance, the Platonic-Socratic doctrine of Ideas.

[2] It may also be compared with W. B. Yeats' remarks on the Glance in sculpture. (*A Vision*, pp. 275-7.)

would here of course demur to Kierkegaard's dogmatic distinction: that *infinite qualitative difference* by which, like some other professors of the " negative theology ", he made all real approach to the Divine impossible. In so far as Christ and His apostles spoke the " fecundating Word ", they were doing essentially the same thing as the Platonic Socrates in his more inspired moments. And if introspection can give us knowledge of the Ideas, it could no less (theoretically) discover the Christian doctrine " Love thy neighbour as thyself ". For what does this in fact mean but that the Other, like the Self, is a Platonic " Idea " or Existential " potency ", and should be held in reverence as such? One imagines Socrates gently forcing modern Existentialists (much against their will!) into the admission. But of course Kierkegaard is not at all primarily concerned with what Jesus taught; what matters to him is the irrational " Paradox ", the atom of the eternal Faery-World inserted into the temporal This-World [1]—no Idea, but " something which would never have entered any man's mind even as a wish or an idea," [2] and hence not discoverable by introspection. This is not merely going beyond any Christian orthodoxy,

---

[1] "The historical fact that God has existed in human form is the essence of the matter; the rest of the historical detail is not even as important as if we had to do with a human being instead of with God. Jurists say that a capital crime submerges all lesser crimes, and so it is with faith. Its absurdity makes all petty difficulties vanish. If the contemporary generation had left nothing behind them but these words, ' We have believed that in such and such a year God appeared among us in the humble figure of a servant, that he lived and taught in our community, and finally died', it would be more than enough."—*Philosophical Fragments*. The language of Karl Barth goes even beyond this, in its almost contemptuous indifference to the Jesus of history: " One whose activity is so easily a little commonplace alongside more than one other founder of a religion, and even alongside many later representatives of his own ' religion' ".—*The Doctrine of the Word of God*. This is not of course to deny that Kierkegaard (in *Works of Love* and elsewhere) gave evidence of a fine Christian spirit, or that Barth is an often moving preacher.

[2] *Journals*.

but it is inconsistent with the better—if I may be so bold, the *æsthetic*—Kierkegaard. If the Incarnation is " Paradox " and " the Offence to Reason "—if the Crucifixion is as senseless as the sacrifice of his son demanded of Abraham, or Jephtha's sacrifice of his daughter, or even Agamemnon's slaughter of Iphigeneia (parallels that haunted Kierkegaard), then the tragedy of Calvary loses, not only intelligibility, but with it all sublimity. However, the poet Kierkegaard was fortunately wiser than the logician. In the very charming fable of the king and the humble maiden [1] (a variant on his eternal theme), he gives us a parable of the Incarnation which anyone with imagination can understand, and (in spite of the strange analogy) accept.

It is indeed typical of Kierkegaard's way of thought that he sees the Incarnation, not as a bridge, but as a *barrier* to the love of God—for the sad pleasure, in his words, of " beating his brow against it till the blood came ". " Offence ", for Kierkegaard, remains a " dialectical factor " in the Divine Love, as despair continues vigorously alive in faith. It is, according to him, " the guarantee whereby God assures Himself that man cannot come too near to Him ".[2] Those who wish may see in this a distrust of religious emotionalism, an attempt to guard the mutual independence of God and the soul; for Kierkegaard always expressed a lively Protestant contempt for the effusions of the mystics. But for him the object of such mutual independence is that both should be unhappy! [3] His wish, never quite relinquished, to live beside Regine in celibate matrimony—a marriage not " mediated " by sense or even sight but only by his stream of printed " discourses "—this oddest of desires, a source (we

---

[1] *Philosophical Fragments.*   [2] *Sickness unto Death.*

[3] " The love of Christ, humanly understood, was not self-sacrificing—anything but that; He did not make Himself unhappy in order, humanly understood, to make His disciples happy. . . . No, humanly speaking, it was indeed madness: *He sacrifices Himself in order to make the beloved equally unhappy with Himself!* "—*Training in Christianity.* (My italics.)

may guess) of no little embarrassment to the lady herself, was increasingly transferred to the Divine Lover. The Abraham became the Isaac—from the active part (if it can be called so in his case) he moved to the passive; but both the sacrifice and the offering are frozen, for him, in an eternal immobility of pain, the eternity of the fabulous " Instant " in which the vulture eviscerates Prometheus. (And there is nothing like pain for stretching out the instant![1]) Kierkegaard became indeed a mystic—perhaps the first mystic of Lutheranism and the last in Christendom—but one who praised the " aridity " or *acedia* of the mystics as the supreme experience. For him, the " flight of the Alone to the Alone " was a flight of parallels that can never touch. Rejecting both reason and *positive* mystical experience, he cut away in fact every ground for faith, bequeathing to a faithless later age his irrational have-it-both-ways *will*. Justifying the famous sneer of Hume, he insisted (with terrible seriousness) that miracles need even greater miracles to be believed.

In thus opposing " faith " to reason, Kierkegaard was being used by the Time-Spirit, even if he was setting himself against the spirit of his own time. It is this " impossibilism " which endears him to very many today for whom the dogma of the Atonement is meaningless or repugnant—which makes him the prototype and patron-saint of the artist-philosophers: unless indeed we go behind him to William Blake, who similarly opposed Imagination to Reason, and identified the former with Jesus. Blake, however, was a man of happy faith—faith such as may one day again be possible to

[1] It is not far from Kierkegaard's thought that *Man*, corporately, crucified Jesus—as Abraham (in intention) sacrificed his son, or as he himself had broken with Regine—in order that the Victim might be rendered back (and yet of course not *wholly* given back, because the sin of Deicide on one side, and the " offence " of Incarnation on the other, must forever preserve the " pathos of distance ").

men [1]; whereas Kierkegaard, despairing of having faith as his fathers knew it, made a strange religion of his despair. Our age, which has mapped the whole continent of disillusionment, sees in him not an apostle, but a Quixote among the pastors and a Hamlet among the Poloniuses of the Enlightenment; his Lutheran God means little to us, but his Dread remains. In Kierkegaard's great but imprisoned soul, as art had remained " the Æsthetic Phase " so mysticism became pietism—but a pietism which fascinates by its pain. It is doubtful whether pain can be pursued for itself without the assistance of self-deception; and I must quote here, as pendent to that already given, another passage from Kierkegaard, in which we may notice, as we are disposed, the contrast—or the arresting similarity:

Behold where he stands—God! Where? There; do you not see him? He is God, and yet he has not a resting-place for his head. . . . How wonderful a life, all sorrow and all love: to yearn to express the equality of love and yet to be misunderstood; to apprehend the danger that all men may be destroyed, and yet only so to be able really to save a single soul. . . . O bitter cup! More bitter than wormwood is the bitterness of death for a mortal, how bitter then for an immortal! O bitter refreshment, more bitter than aloes, to

---

[1] There is of course the Blake of " Experience " as well as the Blake of " Innocence ". One seems to grasp the very quintessence of Kierkegaard in such lines as these:

> " Her fingers number every Nerve,
> Just as a miser counts his gold:
> She lives upon his shrieks and cries,
> And she grows young as he grows old,
>
> " Till he becomes a bleeding youth,
> And she becomes a Virgin bright;
> Then he rends up his Manacles
> And binds her down for his delight."

Compare this with the literally terrifying retelling of the story of Abraham and Isaac in *Fear and Trembling*.

be refreshed by the misunderstanding of the beloved! O solace in affliction to suffer as one who is guilty! What solace then to suffer as one who is innocent![1]

.   .   .   .   .

So far I have attempted to draw the portrait of an unhappy man, of singularly complicated mind: a Swift of the Romantic Era, who wrapped in his fantasy and irony the secrets of a wounded, or self-wounded, heart. But it is certainly not possible at this day (nor, surely, will it ever be) fully to lay bare those secrets, or to pin down that scintillating being under a neat symmetric formula. Kierkegaard forms no mere study in religious, or even literary, psychology. This preacher of obedience was he who fathered, curiously, a doctrine of " total freedom "; this lover forever explaining why he broke his engagement was the man out of whom came the philosophy of " engagement "! Kierkegaard was a butterfly caught in youth in another scintillating, but to most people less attractive, thing, from which he was never completely to disengage himself: namely, the spider's web of Hegel's dialectic. Kierkegaard cannot be understood if we do not understand the achievement of Hegel; yet Hegel is generally as neglected and underrated today as he was once, in Protestant Europe, uncritically accepted. Hegel is the last of the systematic philosophers, as Kierkegaard was (in spite of himself) the first of a new race, the philosopher-artists. Contraries as they are, each of them displays in himself the same contradiction—the contradiction of the age of the Great Revolution. Hegel attempted to view Time *sub specie æternitatis*, and arrived at a sort of mysticism; Kierkegaard thought of Eternity as a shattering Instant—a temporal " leap "—and constructed a queer self-explanatory philosophy. Hegel was a "spoilt" poet, as Kierkegaard was a thinker *manqué*. The one was completely unsociable, and

[1] *Philosophical Fragments.*

yet a public figure; the other was when young (and in a sense always) a man about town, yet led the most exciting inner life ever recorded. But both are, finally, uncomfortable prophets; one searches their biographies in vain for a fellow to Kant's drunken valet Lampe, or even Schopenhauer's poodle!

The system of Hegel, one might perhaps put it, is the greatest monument of the Romantic Movement; though it is no doubt too systematic and too monumental to be altogether " romantic ". Hegel may be called a romantic realist, who took as his presupposition the saying of Plato that the real is the rational, and exhorted his students (in a fine phrase) to be serious with the belief in a divine government of the universe. He had no patience with the talk about this Vale of Tears, this weary *apprentissage* for a Better World, but set about exhibiting the cosmos—in all its Gothic exuberance and variety—as a mighty organic Synthesis and Plan. Such an idea—already implicit in Spinoza, Leibniz and the eighteenth-century deism—was possible in that French-Revolutionary dawn, before industrialism had come to complicate the scene, and when science still was a half-poetical " natural philosophy ". We may hope that it may, as an attitude at least, be again possible, when the activisms of today shall have " collapsed " (in Hegel's sensational phrase) into their harmonious synthesis. (That metaphor of collapsing upward gives us a hint, perhaps, of Hegel's worst mistake: the automatisation of living processes.) For the Romantics were attempting (with bits of Plato, the myths of all races then known, and the Cabbalistic doctrines) to find a substitute for dogmatic Christianity: a substitute, or re-creation, which a secularised Europe most sorely needs. But they were too impatient, too scornful of the Christian tradition, too little aware of the rising clamour of the masses; and their whole energy was finally appropriated (in a typical " dialectical " somersault) by the inverted Hegelianism of Marx.

For if Marxists (and most Existentialists) believe too much in Action, Hegel believed too much in Logic; but in logic of a very peculiar kind. I have compared him to the Deists and Rationalists, but of course Hegel went farther back, to the mystics and Gnostics: only, the God which they *felt after* in the beginnings of Time, he *thought* his way towards at its end. Identifying Thought and Time, he made Thought concrete and Time abstract—a ceaseless joining and dividing of concepts. The end of both processes, the Divine Thought and Thinker, was the same—namely perfect Man on Earth; even though it looked a little like the perfect German! Such a system was indeed a mental Festival-of-Reason—a first metaphysical sketch of Evolution, as well as a final bringing-down-to-earth of the mystic's dream. It may indeed fitly be compared with the Tower of Babel, which doubtless had no fault as a work of art or engineering except that it was too ambitious. The skeleton of that System was the winding stair of the *Dialectic*—a logic not of Being but of Becoming, not of deduction but of development. One might call it (as no one that I am aware has done) an Existential Logic; and in fact all Existentialists build with its ruins. Hegel offered to deduce from *blue* and *yellow* (let us say for simplicity), not the mere tautology *blue and yellow*, but the synthesis—a new concreteness—*green;* and he applied this mode of " re-thinking the thought of God "—or believed that it could, given the time, be applied—to everything in the universe, from the unfolding of the Spring vegetation to the succession of schools in art [1]. With one significant exception, however: Hegel stopped before the Future. He was too much of a nineteenth-century German to conceive that the Protestant monarchical order he knew would ever duly " collapse ", with its contrary, into a " higher synthesis "; he was also,

---

[1] Marx's collaborator Engels, after devoting seven years to this attempt (naturally with a partisan purpose), concluded sadly that the task was too great for one man.

it should be said, too honest a philosopher to indulge in wishful prophecy. But this rather glaring *lacuna* clearly falsified the whole scheme. For if History was to be viewed, not *sub specie æternitatis* but *sub specie anni 1807* (the year when the *Phenomenology* was published), then clearly the Past would appear in a very false, arbitrary, perspective [1]; and if the Dialectic were a reliable instrument, then the Future should have been predictable, at least in broad outlines—a consequence which for Marx, and for some German chauvinists,[2] constituted almost the whole of its charm. It was clear —as Kierkegaard in substance, and with lively sarcasm, pointed out—that Hegel's edifice lacked the top storey; and that a theory which left one beside the road, with no signposts, was not a very useful or trustworthy machine.

What is the truth about this *Dialectic*, which has since produced so much grandiloquent thought, bad writing and demented action: which is today (in a debased form, it is true) an article of faith over a fifth of the globe? If there is anything in it (and I believe there is a great deal in it), it is surely time that all serious thinkers should ask themselves the question. Kierkegaard said that if Hegel had proposed the *Logic* as a *hypothesis* merely, he would be remembered as the greatest of human minds; and though this was of course a *boutade*, it makes us realise a little of Hegel's impact upon another, and not sympathetic, great mind. It would seem clear that if the Dialectic is mathematically exact, it must be a discovery as important, at least, as the greatest

[1] It is a Sartrian thesis that our present decisions not only influence the farthest future, but can even be said to alter the past—by altering its meaning and direction: that, in fact, the past is what we choose to make it. This hardly squares with Sartre's ultra-" realistic " assertion that " Evil cannot be redeemed." (See page 12.)

[2] To make Hegel responsible—as is often done—for German nationalism, and even National Socialism, is, however, quite unjust. Hegel's influence in Germany sank to vanishing-point almost at once after his death, and had no come-back. Since then, his chief followers and interpreters have been fierce-eyed Scotsmen and dynamic Italians.

discoveries of physical science; if it is altogether fantastic—
a " Red Indian myth ", as the French thinker Brunschvicg
called it—it must be as baneful a superstition as ever plagued
humanity. I believe it is neither quite true nor quite false,
but marks the limit and (in Existentialist language) " checkmate " to all philosophy, its necessary failure to hold the
fluid element of Time in its abstract weighing-scales, the
flaw in metaphysics which must forever prevent its becoming
an exact science. Actually, Hegel's initial triad of *Being—
Nothing—Becoming* represents almost all that is still interesting
and valuable in the Great System; as soon as the plot thickens
and the reality becomes more complex, the scheme no longer
fits. Hutchison Stirling, in a now little read work *The
Secret of Hegel*, announced the Secret thus: " As Aristotle
(with assistance from Plato) made explicit the *abstract*
Universal that was implicit in Socrates, so Hegel (with less
considerable assistance from Fichte and Schelling) made
explicit the *concrete* Universal that was implicit in Kant."
Which is, no doubt, true and important. Hegel took the
Kantian paraphernalia of Thought—somewhat as Aristotle
took the Platonic paraphernalia of Forms—strung them,
like coloured disks, on the electric wire of Development-in-
Time, and made them (only much faster!) gyrate. However,
the Thing-in-Itself of Kant was a Mystery, and the Concrete
Universal of Hegel is (strictly) a mystification: for universals
are abstractions, and there are no words for the individual
which alone is concrete, and which Hegel consistently
disdained. Kierkegaard, who remained essentially a Hegelian,
was only pushing the " identity of contraries " to its conclusion when he preached (absurdly, I think) what he called
the " Paradox " or the " Absurd ". It was a desperate
attempt to save by Hegelian reason what, for ordinary
reason, he already himself regarded as a lost cause; for in
that age the Christian position seemed more hopeless than
(in the view of many) it seems today. Yet the moment we

start to think concretely we are really passing from philosophy to poetry, from description to revelation, from the
statable to the merely suggestible: and, I should say—if I
may make so bold as to contradict Kierkegaard—from
theology to poetry too. If the logic of Aristotle and his
predecessors was the birth of Western philosophy, the
" logic " of Hegel represents its death: the crossing-over of
speculation into what you can call (and the Master himself
sometimes called) mysticism. Hegel failed; his " concrete
thought " has remained still-born, and no Hegelian has ever
succeeded in revitalising it. But Hegel's failure was the
ultimate failure of metaphysics, and after him there has been
no metaphysician in the great style. Like the mythical
Tower, the philosophical effort has failed through the
ambiguities of words; for words are both too instinct with
life to be given mathematically fixed meanings, and too
lifeless to correspond with any exactness to reality.[1] (For
instance, Hegel's writing, with its many solemn puns, loses
much of its plausibility when read in translation; and this
is even truer of our second subject, Heidegger.) The
Dialectic, like alchemy and astrology, can give us very
valuable hints and poetic insights, and suggest real elements
of pattern in life and development; but let us beware of
making a magic science out of it! The Dialectic is Pegasus—
and it is the Nightmare, if anyone but a poet ride her: for
her masters must be not merely metaphysicians, but must
possess physical flair and tact. With this servant a mere
theorist will come near to destroying the world, like Marx:
or will destroy himself, as Kierkegaard almost did.

Kierkegaard, I repeat, remained entirely Hegelian in his
way of thought. With him, as he once said, all is dialectical;

[1] There is another reason for Hegel's partial failure—namely that the
Dialectic has more movements than one, as Croce was the first to perceive (*What is Living and What is Dead of the Philosophy of Hegel*). I offer
some suggestions of my own in an Appendix to this book.

guilt, despair, remorse, anguish—everything in his burdened and stricken life goes like a ballet. Nevertheless, in spirit, of course, he reacted from " the System " with the utmost vehemence. His critique of Hegelianism is still of the very greatest interest: even though the particular mood of Hegel is far removed (at least in appearance) from the age we live in. He attacked it as Samuel Butler attacked Darwinism, or as Ruskin attacked the Manchester School—largely for the very reason that it was a system: Thesis-and-Antithesis, like Variation-and-Selection or Supply-and-Demand, seemed to have substituted an industrial process for the grandeur and pathos of the human will. Yet if Darwinians and Laissez-Fairists made their sciences lisp in English, Hegel (as he boasted) made philosophy speak German; and it was no idle boast! In his prose, the bewildering habits of the German language reach a climax; verbs split in half and re-combine as if charged with terrible life, prepositions and particles heave and thrust like piston-rods, monosyllables conglomerate like globules of water into crashing cascades. And the language was the reflexion of the content; Hegelianism is the very spirit of excessiveness. " The real ", said Hegel, " is the Bacchic delirium, in which there is not one of its components which is not drunk "; and certainly there was not one of his pupils who did not share the delirium. Kierkegaard, who in youth had drunk deep of that heady brew, was the first to suffer a " hangover " and to abjure the revels. He declared his revolt by a phrase on which Hegel had visited particular scorn: the familiar Teutonism—title of Kierkegaard's first considerable work—to wit, *Either/Or*.

For Hegel's monistic philosophy, all sharp alternatives were " abstract " and ultimately unreal; their difference was in fact their identity.[1] They were the " antithetical "

---

[1] It might be said that as Kierkegaard saw the Mediator as a necessary barrier or " stumbling-block ", so Hegel saw every barrier as a bridge, all negation as mediation. Even supposing Hegel could have been

rivulets of which the " concrete universal ", like a majestic river, was composed. And it was a ceaselessly expanding river; for each successive phase gathered up and incorporated fresh contributory streams. Hegel, as we have seen, combined by a brilliant *tour de force* the secular doctrine of Progress with the mystic's Vision of the One; and though we may agree that the goal of history is a vision of truth, we cannot equate history with the nineteenth-century's " Progress ", or Truth with any System. For Hegel, art and religion were two unrealities until merged in their " Ground ", philosophy; the family and society were a pair of abstractions, waiting to be " overcome " by their synthesis, the modern State. Sin (though one-sided and therefore " unreal ") was a higher phase than the innocence which precedes it: every Fall was a " blessed crime ", with the accent upon the " blessed "—a *reculer pour mieux sauter*. Such a conception seemed to Kierkegaard merely an immoral æstheticism, a cosmic " Try-everything-once " doctrine, a justification of all the possible Means as leading to a fixed and pre-established good End: namely the egotistic Self-Realisation of the Absolute. Kierkegaard, who had been what Hegel never was, an æsthete—dreaming with the Romantics of expanding his personality, of achieving an Olympian or Faustian universalism—Kierkegaard hungered for real decisions. In the language of the later Existentialism, he longed for a real *engagement*. While retaining the Hegelian scheme of Three Stages, he joined it—not perhaps very happily—to a stern Protestant dualism. The æstheticophilosophic stage (except as a necessary jumping-off ground) was Bad, the ethical and religious stages were Good; and the

caught out in an error (and there was obviously no test by which you could catch him), he would have defended himself by saying " Error is a necessary dialectical factor in truth ". (But it would be equally hard to pin down Kierkegaard to a real belief. It might always be a mere logical paradox, put forward to exercise our will-to-faith—as God, according to some anti-Darwinians, put the fossils in the mountains.)

ethical also (as for Luther) seemed more and more to figure on the wrong side of the ledger. The idea—essentially a right one—of the highest life as a *Synthesis* disappeared; or it was replaced, at least, by that of an " armed truce ".

I have said that Kierkegaard, in my opinion, here undervalued philosophy. But Hegel, on his side, had immoderately exalted it. He saw the philosopher as " higher " than the creative artist or the saint—because taking in, with his sweeping glance, the whole of reality, of which they (men of practice only) were but parts. The Hegelian " logic " was supposedly a re-thinking of the thought of Creation—whereas it was obviously no more than a manipulation of concepts, which other men had first discovered by the use of quite ordinary logic. And this led to a peculiar mental vice—of a kind known to late sleepers, who are dimly aware, through their dreams, that it is time they should be up. It may be called the vice of thinking you have done a thing, when you have in fact only imagined or dreamt it. The Hegelian really thought that when he had " posited " an idea, and then " negated " it, and negated the negation— when he had " broken down " these two contraries into their " synthesis " (as in the game where you " take away the number you first thought of ")—that when he had compassed this little gambit he was a sort of alchemist producing gold in his alembic. Whereas of course (in this, probably like the alchemist) he had done almost nothing at all—far, far less than the primitive savage who first, by the magic of names, distinguished the concepts " water " and " fire ", or the day from the night.

This Hegelian fallacy, as I have put it, may seem too patently absurd ever to have blinded intelligent people. Actually it corresponds to a very common, almost universal, modern trick of thought. The modern man lives for the most exciting part of his experience in an unreal film-world, intercalated between himself and the real world—a film-

world of which the humble street-corner " Pictures " are
merely the external symbol—an idealist world of " repre-
sentations " and " appearances ", with the " things in
themselves " forgotten or conjured away. He knows that in
his acts he is a pawn; in his dreams, on the other hand, he is
a magician—an omnipotence! Like a night-walking Caliph
of Baghdad, he can encounter all possible experiences in,
so to speak, their ideal essence, untarnished by the dirt and
heat of reality. He can " concretise " himself, with the
facility of a spirit, as a Casanova, a Danton or a Florence
Nightingale; he can pose (or " posit ") each of them in turn;
" annul " them by comparison, one with another; finally
" rescue " them in a higher synthesis—to wit, his ironical
sophisticated self. Containing them all, he can take them
out at will like a ventriloquist, and converse with them in a
tone of condescending familiarity—or, speaking through
their mouths, set them to talk with each other. And all the
time he is not only much less than any one of them (as I—I
shall very rightly be told—am less than giants like Kierkegaard and Hegel), but he is, or would seem in any other age,
scarcely a man at all! Rather he is, in a useful contemporary
phrase, a depersonalised " ghost in a machine ". Well, it
is not necessary to abuse the modern man, in the style of a
Belloc or a Lawrence. There is something of worth in his
critical universalism, his diversified popular culture; there
is *something*, after all, in Progress. Contemplation (though
the modern man's self-conscious virility will not let him
admit it) is indeed, in the end, higher than action. But the
point here is that it tends to mean living at second-hand, and
the Hegelian logic (in Hegel's followers, and in large tracts
of Hegel himself) was a cerebration at second-hand—a kind
of philosophical chess with only one player, and in which all
the moves are knight's moves—a " re-thinking " and not a
first thinking. The System had no *words of command*—no
answer to the question " What shall I do to be saved? ", or

46

even to the more modest enquiry " What am I to do next ? "[1]
In Kierkegaard's terms, it could not rise above the " Interesting " and the " Possible ". Hegel's block-universe might
be right, approximatively, for Omniscience [2]; for a nineteenth-century professor it was a bourgeois pretence, like
the mansion of a new rich.

It was thus, at least, that Kierkegaard saw it. Hegelian
idealism seemed to him merely an inflated materialism,
excluding all " transcendences "—both God and human
freedom. It excluded them for the very reason that it
attempted to merge and sink them in a single whole—in a
concept or " notion ", or (to give it the forbidding German
name) a *Begriff*. Kierkegaard could have said of Hegel what

[1] " In spite of all that Hegel says about process, he does not understand history from the point of view of becoming, but with the help of
the illusion attaching to pastness understands it from the point of view
of a finality that excludes all becoming. It is therefore impossible for a
Hegelian to understand himself by means of his philosophy, for his
philosophy helps him to understand only that which is past and finished,
and a living person is surely not dead. He probably finds compensation
in the thought that in comparison with an understanding of China and
Persia and 6,000 years of the world's history, a single individual does not
much matter, even if that individual be himself. But it seems otherwise
to me, and I understand it better conversely; when a man cannot understand himself, his understanding of China and Persia and the rest must
surely be of a very peculiar kind." *Concluding Unscientific Postscript*.

[2] " Reality itself is a system—for God; but it cannot be a system for
any existing spirit. System and finality correspond to one another, but
existence is precisely the opposite of finality . . . Existence separates,
and holds the various moments of existence discretely apart; the
systematic thought consists of the finality which brings them together."
—*Concluding Unscientific Postscript*. As applied to Hegel, all this partly
misses its mark. Hegel insisted very much on the heterogeneity of
historic moments and the necessity of decision (*Entscheidung*)—though
for nations and leaders rather than for private individuals. " Every
people is in such an individual situation that it must and will decide
for itself. . . . No general principle, no memory of similar circumstances,
is of any help in the press of world-events."—*Die Vernunft in der
Geschichte*. The danger of such doctrine is evident; but Kierkegaard was
not at all troubled by what is nowadays called the immoralistic side of
Hegel.

Pascal said of Descartes, " Why, he would take me for a proposition! " And this leads us to the second great vice in Hegelianism, which consisted in being hypnotised by what has happened, as a hen is said to be hypnotised by a chalk-line; for the Past, whether seen as glorious or not-so-glorious, is always " rational "—in the sense of being a complex of effects and causes. Hegelianism was a meta-physical Success-doctrine—a sort of Natural Selection applied to ideas. For Hegel, every real value in the dialectical evolution was necessarily translated, perfectly and com-pletely, into actuality; as the world itself was the perfectly adequate representation of Thought.[1] There were no unrealised or unrealisable perfections—there was no possible Might-be or Ought-to-be or If-only. Hegel was the bitter opponent of all idealism, in the popular meaning of the word which goes back to Plato—the alleged superiority of the Dream to the Fact, the view of this world as the faint or blurred reflexion of a better one. He hated all world-betterers and, as the current term is, escapists. His concep-tion was nearer to that of Aristotle, who held that the " ideas " were essences or potencies tending towards actualisation. In all this he was attempting, commendably, to abolish dualism—the traditional Platonic-Christian cleft

[1] It is important to remember that when Kierkegaard says " Sub-jectivity is truth " he is not, like some of his followers, attacking the scientific outlook. Doubtless he cared nothing for science; but in his youth science was scarcely yet " exact " science. It had not yet dis-solved its ancient partnership with philosophy; and for Kierkegaard, we have seen, philosophy meant Hegelianism. It was Hegel's rather mis-leading identification of " objectivity " with thought (meaning the self-generating, extremely subjective, Hegelian thought) that drove Kierke-gaard to an equally unfortunate assault on reason itself in the name of subjectivity (by which he meant a quite objective belief in the Gospel facts). And I should add that if the Existentialists here follow Kierkegaard's bad example, the Marxists follow that of Hegel. For them, by an incred-ible perversion of language, a crime can be " objectively " meritorious —meaning, within the context of the class-struggle, or more simply, if it is useful to the Party.

between Matter and Spirit. Dualism, however, cannot be cured by logic, even by so unorthodox a logic as the Hegelian one; for all logic implies the separation between a knower and a known. A mystic would deny the " real " world, a materialist the ideal: an " idealist " like Hegel simply christens the Real " Spirit " or " Idea ", and thinks he has closed the gap. Actually, Hegel would admit imperfection only where romantic poets have taught us to see a relative perfection: namely in the realm of Nature. Nature was the domain of *Chance*, from which human dreams and aspirations were a sort of overspill or vegetable excrescence. To rate dreams above actualities seemed to him like preferring an artist's first shadowy conception to the finished picture or statue. He was perhaps not enough of an artist to realise that in every first conception there is an element that, irrecoverably, escapes; something is won in the execution, but something also is forfeited.[1] Something is sacrificed in every progress or perfectioning—even if, haply, more is gained. And the beauties of Nature, to which Hegel was insensitive, are to some beings moving because they are elusive—like the myriad unfinished fantasies of a prodigal genius. The true " synthesis " is not represented, as the later Hegel might have seen it, by a statesman unveiling a monument on a national holiday, but by those rare and fleeting moments when the thought and the hand seem to run in unison, with almost the purity of chance: moments when (in an unusually optimistic phrase of Kierkegaard) one can be happy afloat over 70,000 fathoms, and when what romantics call " the World " is for the moment well lost.[2]

[1] " Interiority is never fully expressed in any action."—KIERKEGAARD. This is the root both of the Kierkegaardian " irony " and " anguish ".

[2] For all that, Hegel was, as I have suggested, more of an artist than has been common among philosophers, as his system is fundamentally an æsthetic product—indeed a romantic one. In fact, the contrast between the later and the earlier (Schellingist) Hegel would illustrate my very point. This unfortunately led, as we have seen, to Kierkegaard's bracketing of philosophy with æstheticism.

This may seem obvious to the point of banality; but the error in question is, again, one which has deeply permeated our thinking. At no time, I have said, has man been freer and less constrained in his dreams and notions; and the antithesis to this thesis is that never has he felt less free in acts. The perfect synthesis of these positions is in fact the totalitarian State, in which he regains the sense of freedom of action—by merging himself in a collective notion or dream. This is the final extreme of " historic logic ", and one scarcely believes that Hegel would have liked it; but the whole atmosphere of the age is soaked in this metaphysical fatalism. Catholic writers commonly attribute it to materialism, but Kierkegaard would have seen it, more truly, as the product of " idealism "; it is fundamentally a religious belief in *process*, which is dangerous because it is near to a great truth.[1] Whenever people say that this thing or that " had to come " or " has come to stay " or " has time on its side ", they are in fact talking, without knowing it, a popularised Hegelianism; they are assuming more rationality in the course of events than there is, or than can ever be discovered. Kierkegaard remarked (as a motto for Danish thinkers) that there were many things in heaven and earth undreamed of in German philosophy: the first of them, one might add, is that earth is not heaven. In the terms of modern Existentialism, *Existence* can never be *Essence*; and the attempt to bring them together is the absurdity which is, so to speak, the self-contradictory " essence " of Existence.

To all this, Hegel would have had an answer, and a very strong one; it is an answer which, it seems to me, has received too little attention. Whether or not Hegel should be called a religious man, he was, at any rate, deeply interested in

[1] " In the world-historical process God is metaphysically imprisoned in a conventional strait-jacket, half metaphysical and half æsthetic-dramatic, that is, the immanential system. It must be the very devil to be God in that manner."—*Concluding Unscientific Postscript.*

50

religion, which he placed even above art on his dialectical ladder. He had in youth had propensities to mysticism, and had written a life of Christ. He regarded himself in fact as the interpreter of Christianity to the new age; though orthodox Christians, from Kierkegaard downwards, have angrily rejected his claim. The Christian religion, as Hegel could (and did) point out, has made Man—in the Person of Jesus—the perfect and adequate concretisation of God-head. The religion of Christ is called the crown and fulfil-ment of the Mosaic monotheism precisely for this reason. Hegel could even refer to shadowy hints in the mystics of *three* historic Dispensations—with a promised Kingdom of the Holy Ghost to follow those of the Father and Son; and to a German, *Geist* usually means Spirit in the sense of Mind—the very meaning of the Hegelian " concrete universal ". Hegel could maintain that if the God-Man (or concrete Mind) were equal or superior to the absolute Godhead, so History in Time must be equal or superior to any static " ideal " or Idea-world. And he supported this contention by a new version, or inversion, of the famous Ontological Argument—an argument which may be called the great puzzle of Western philosophy. If the argument is sound, philosophy is wrong; and if it is unsound, theology is wrong. The Ontological Argument, it will be remembered, sets out to prove God from the thought of Him, or His Existence from His Essence. Kant showed clearly that it was the only substantial proof of His existence, and, equally clearly, that it was fallacious. And in so doing, it may be said incidentally, Kant opened that chasm between Exist-ence and Essence which is the special theme, or obsession, of the Existentialists. And yet the famous Proof haunts and fascinates us, as the Irrational Number haunted the intellect of Greece. If we can *think* Perfection (so we feel) surely that Perfection must, somehow or somewhere, exist. Hegel in effect replied, " Yes, it exists in the total view of Reality.

Since everything less than the Whole is imperfect, the Whole alone is Perfection, and in thinking it I am nothing less than God ". The Ontological Argument could be phrased, " I think God, therefore God is". Hegel, in substance, amended it, " I think God, therefore I am God ".

Nietzsche said that God was dead; for Hegel, it will be seen, He had in fact been reborn—as Man. This teaching of Hegel's was like the disclosure of some terrible secret; for it seemed to justify at a stroke all the evil in the world. Good and Evil were the light and shade in the picture, alike necessary for the pleasure of the philosophic beholder. Or rather, the contemplator must be responsive— through his " lower ", non-visual, senses—to the shadowed side of Being. That second eye of the Cosmos, the Night, reclaimed its rights. The world was perfect not merely *in spite of* the evil in it (that " best possible world " of Leibniz) but *because of* it; for without the element of contradiction there would be no change, motion or, in short, life. Nevertheless I believe, as I have said, that such an *æsthetic* acceptance of the Cosmos is the only possible one—now that those other, "better", worlds have faded; and that this is the only serious answer to that " problem of evil ", which the older philosophies really had burked or despaired of solving. Supernatural faith had been like the comfort given to a child that " Father knows best " or " You will understand when you are older " (to drop the simile, it meant " You will understand after you are dead "); Hegel was the first to announce, like a child coming to the uses and misuses of reason, " Now I see ". To accept the world and time as a perfect artistic whole may seem a large order—calling, certainly, for the help of faith; but it is clear that the larger a work of art or architecture, the more rubble and chaos it must contain—a sonnet can be exquisite in every line, but scarcely an epic. However, if we do not feel *dread*—and, as Kierkegaard did, an instinctive revolt—before such a belief, we are unmoral æsthetes merely; and Hegel, perhaps, did not feel the dread or the revolt. He tended to stress his rather maddening, unvarying, metre in every line of the Great Poem; to stretch his " diamond web " of dialectic till it snapped—and the diamonds had an unauthentic look. It is doubtful, indeed, if a man endowed with normal sensibilities and disgusts (including self-disgust) could have elaborated the notion. For Hegel, after all, was the inheritor of an over-rationalised Christianity. His paradigm started with *Pure Being*—a remnant of the Scholastic *Pure Act*; he found no place for Boehme's *Ungrund*, the " Abyss " of potentiality—a doctrine lately revived by Berdyaev, which corresponds in fact to the " Nothing " of Heidegger and Sartre.[1] " Nothing ", for him, was a simple undulation —not a sheer breach of continuity. He did not feel Negation (the world under the Minus Sign) as something frighteningly tangible, like a face that we feel, with our fingers, in the dark.

Kierkegaard thought he was rebelling against Hegel, whereas he—and the Existentialists who have followed him—were only bringing out the implications of the Negative. That " Dark God " Subjectivity, which Hegel had set free, was magnified by Kierkegaard and his followers into the very God—the archetypal Abraham raising the knife to slay his son, the perpetual revolt of our Freedom against the bonds of Causality and Law.[2] The Kierkegaard-

---

[1] Sartre would deny this, since he approaches the question as a phenomenologist and not as a mystic. For him as for Descartes, speculation begins with human subjectivity; he does not, like most of the Germans, assume an Absolute. " It is man ", he says, " who causes the Nothing to be ". Nevertheless he associates the Nothing with the Will, which "gnaws " at Being like a worm in a fruit; and the Sartrian Will— a " useless passion "—is very near to the Schopenhauerian Will (the " Desire " of Eastern mysticism) which creates the illusion of a world.

[2] It may assist the reader if he keeps in mind that the rather forbidding term *Nothing*, in Existentialist writing, corresponds almost always to human subjectivity, " existence ", or primordial freedom (mental concepts being included, along with *things*, under Being or " essence "—

ian antithesis, like the Hegelian thesis, was still within the Christian frame of reference; Kierkegaard upheld the logical contradiction—the Suffering God—against Hegel's assertion of logical unity in the concrete God. But it was in fact the ancient contest of volition against cognition—exemplified (in a less degree) by Pascal versus Descartes, Duns Scotus versus Aquinas,[1] Heraclitus versus the Eleatics, by Jerusalem versus Athens and Geneva versus Rome. (This is so, even though the contest is itself, of course, full of contradictions and ambivalences. Thus Kierkegaard at times seems like a Catholic criticising Protestant Hegel; for Kierkegaard's indifference to the *historical* Jesus, and to the " progressive Revelation ", strikes one as more Catholic than Protestant.) In opposition to Hegel's ideal philosopher, the *knowing* man, Kierkegaard set up the *willing* or *suffering* man; for the two ideas are of course the same, and are combined in the ambiguous term *wanting*.[2] And we must grant that Hegelianism is wrong without the corrective of Kierkegaardianism. The world is not only a " ballet ot categories ", a comedy of *essences*—though it is that as well. It is also a tragic strife between *existences*—not least when man is alone, between the two souls which (as Goethe said) inhabit his breast. It is tragic for the very reason that they are two, and can never (in *this* world, Kierkegaard would

for concepts are objective inasmuch as I *think* them). To call the human subject a " Nothing " would seem less paradoxical if the term were always written " No-thing." It is the *incompleteness* (in Heidegger's language, the *openness*) of the Self which the Existentialists wish to stress.

[1] Kierkegaard's doctrine of a " suspension of the ethical " is virtually a return to the Scotist position that a thing is right or wrong because God wills it so (as opposed to the Thomist one that God wills what is good), and that therefore it can change its character by a decision of the same will.

[2] " The soul ", said Kierkegaard, " is stronger than the whole world by its weakness, and it is weaker than God by its strength." Here, it seems to me, he is speaking of the will. (I owe this striking quotation, which I have been unable to trace, to Jean Wahl's great book *Etudes Kierkegaardiennes*.)

54

have said) attain to a lasting harmony. The boundary between " heaven " and " earth "—between essence and existence—is the Intuition; and it is both a uniting and a dividing line. Hegel regarded it from one point of view, and called all evil " mediation "; Kierkegaard looked at it in the opposite manner, and called separateness " anguish ". The first gave a gospel to æsthetic epicureans, the second founded a queer new school of stoics—the Existentialists. But since their time we have all lived on the farther, " existential ", side of the barrier, and look back to the static *Ancien Régime* of reason and law as to a lost Eden; for to have defined a limit (as Hegel and Kierkegaard defined it) is already to have passed it. That " Existence precedes Essence " is true of our situation today, for those of us who have come out of the tidy hierarchised garden of Plato and the historic Church. If Hegel was the Tempter in that Eden, Kierkegaard is the angel in the gateway, with the two-edged sword. He who summons us back to it prevents our ever truly returning—by that faith of his which does not convince us, his despair which was partly willed, and by the irony which could hold these two " moments " in a not uncomplacent balance.

Kierkegaard—who liked to quote the saying in *King Lear*, " So we'll live . . . as if we were God's spies "[1]—had in fact a rather over-developed taste for irony and mystification. Rather oddly, he was able to read a form of *humour* into the Gospel text (a text contrasting so strongly with his own teaching): " My yoke is gentle and my burden is light." His works—and not only the pseudonymous ones—must be

[1] Kierkegaard was here of course, while addressing his father, speaking in the character of Cordelia. It is significant that in the *Diary of the Seducer*, which reflects (and naturally distorts) Kierkegaard's relations with Regine, he should have chosen the name Cordelia for his heroine. Kierkegaard's " infinite incommensurability between the divine and the human " was the extrapolation of a passion thwarted both on the filial and the sexual planes.

read warily; regarding his life as a play, he thought always really less of truth than of dramatic appropriateness. And as the drama was largely an inner one, we can never possess all the " cues ". Like Hamlet, he treated his Ophelia with a cold brutality—to make her believe (as he pretended) that his love had been a pretence, but probably (as we may surmise) because he himself would have liked to think it so.[1] In his extravagant attacks on the Danish Church, he seems in fact to have been courting a quite chimerical martyrdom; and his motives were as much histrionic as divine. Kierkegaard's religiousness was of course, in the ordinary sense, sincere—even deadly sincere; nevertheless one feels in him a faint but disconcerting likeness to that Calvinistic immoralist, André Gide. There is a thin but real thread which connects the " irrational leap " and the " suspension of the ethical " with the " gratuitous crime ". Both men seem to incarnate the very soul of self-contradiction. Gide was an æsthete who could explore, by way of a change, the anguish of the *Porte Etroite*; Kierkegaard was a mystic, one of whose *alter egos* was Johannes the Seducer. Kierkegaard, like Gide, could only imagine the sensual as the Satanic; Gide, like Kierkegaard, was a " confessional " writer—essentially concerned with the theology of Grace and Freewill. Both of them (though in rather different senses, it is true) made their own the text " Woman, what have I to do with thee? " And Gide's Pauline motto, *Si le Grain ne Meurt*, seems like an echo of the Kierkegaardian " repetition ". The Hegelian law of development, of which the essence is dialectical change, used often to be made a justification for " romantic irony "—for the protean metamorphoses of the " artist in life "; but Hegel's nature had little of irony or play, and the person, for " the System ",

[1] Perhaps also because—his mind obsessed with the " Offence " of the Incarnation—he wanted to test whether Regine would be *offended* by this travesty of his true nature and feelings.

56

was himself no more than a *persona* or mask, temporarily assumed by the World-Spirit—by the " Objective Reason ". Kierkegaard, in his emphasis on the person, thought he was rescuing the earnestness and realism of tragedy; but in another view, he was freeing the individual player from the discipline and oppression of that Hegelian World-Drama— he was creating " Hegelian Man "! Hegel had admired great men (in the public sense), as "moments in God's biography "; but Kierkegaard sometimes came near to the blasphemous theory (a recurrent one in the history of heresy) that God had become incarnate in Jesus as a deliberate disguise.[1] He could almost have said, like the cynical Bishop Blougram:

> Some think, Creation's meant to show Him forth:
> I say, it's meant to hide Him all it can,
> And that's what all the blessed evil's for.

. . . . .

Kierkegaard is praised for his wit and for his beauty of style; and it is true one is constantly made aware of both, even in translation. Yet he is a most exasperating writer; if I were sentenced to solitary confinement, it is not his works I would like to take with me, for the very prison walls would seem more hospitable. He was perhaps almost great enough to do without other people—but certainly he *did* forgo them, more than any writer one can think of. He lived always, one fancies, among his father's imaginary interlocutors, in a ventriloquist's world of puppets, like his own medley of pseudonyms—as Blake ended by living with " Urizen " and the other spectres. Hegel, he said, did not *inhabit* his philosophic mansion; Kierkegaard inhabited his,

[1] Kierkegaard even toys with a still more extreme " paradox "— namely that God, during His Incarnation, might have remained altogether unknown. But in that case (he concludes, with signs of great mental distress) God would be the supreme ironist and no more. Here, perhaps, one will not find it difficult to agree with him.

but it remained a cloud-world still. His wit is fevered and breathless, often close to tears; his descriptions of Nature (though frequently very evocative) are abstract and hyper-lyrical, with no feeling for the homely earth. Nature herself for Kierkegaard, as for some of the German romantics, is " under sin "; the whole Creation shivers like a conscious bride. His enormous sense of a personal guilt strikes us today as near to " Byronism ".[1] Yet precisely because his father's house is so vivid to us, we follow him—as we do Emily Brontë—with fascination: he made, in a sense, " a heaven of hell "—of all the hells that lie about us in our infancy. We understand him better than the saints, just because he was half an artist, and suffered a tension that is of our age: not simply the weary tension of soul and body, but the tension between a man's two souls. What this Christian brought back to Europe was not so much Jerusalem as Greece—the Greece of Æschylus and not of Plato: the ambiguity in human action whereby crime can be sacrificial and the blessings of Fate a curse. He made the Hegelian wire-play tremble, with all the tremors of human nerves; and as he shuddered before his Father, we shudder a little at that tortured player, whose pain brought the play to life.

[1] Many will ask, what was Kierkegaard repenting of? It is clear that he suffered few pangs of conscience, in the ordinary sense—none certainly for his treatment of Regine; it was rather his pride that was hurt, and doubly hurt by her marriage to Schlegel. Kierkegaard had little cause to fear his flesh; and, like many of his contemporaries, he romanticised seducers and demoniacals. Though he ended as a moralist—abusing almost everyone—he cannot be acquitted of self-righteousness. The answer to the riddle is contained, I think, in one of his most famous sayings: "The opposite of sin is not virtue, it is faith." Conversely the opposite of faith is sin. It was faith that Kierkegaard lacked.

II

SYNOPSIS: HEIDEGGER

The character of Kierkegaard's thought ensured its neglect during the Age of Progress. Nevertheless, its anti-intellectualist tendency was akin to some trends of the time. It was reserved for Heidegger, after the first world war, to endeavour to build an existential system; but this is really a contradictory aim, since existence is (in Heidegger's own phrase) an " openness ". Hence the thinness and bleakness of Heidegger's language, recalling that of some Alexandrian doctors of the via negativa. It conveys, however, with genuine power, and as no other philosophy has conveyed, the mystery and omnipresence of Nonentity.

Heidegger began his career as a pupil of Husserl, a mathematical thinker, who attempted to reduce objects and subjective states alike to the status of " ideas "; consciousness, for Husserl, was a mere pointer or " intention "—when I feel, I feel my feeling. Heidegger read into such " intentionality " the pathos of the Will, the Kierkegaardian Dread—not, however, before God, but before Nothingness. Heidegger—like Kierkegaard, and in a different way like Husserl—revolted against both idealism and materialism; with him, the Self is the centre, but the Self's nature is to be in a " situation ". Husserl had advanced his system as a methodology merely; he " bracketed " (set aside) the whole question of existence. Heidegger, however, saw existence itself as a Husserlian " intention ", which he renamed " projection "—towards an object in the future. That object is, in the final analysis, Death; Heidegger is not (as he has been called) an " idealist ", but in fact a nihilist. For Heidegger, Life (because it must end) is Sorge (Care or Sorrow) and Schuld (Indebtedness, also Guilt)—terms which he employs, not quite ingenuously, for their religious resonance. Man is " living

59

*authentically " when he looks forward bravely to his death; we can
agree—though again, Heidegger's moral nihilism scarcely warrants
this language. Heidegger makes the point that all men, half unconsciously, hope to escape death; but he does not show (as he might)
that endless life would be the true misery. Nor does he favour
quietism or detachment: the Heideggerian hero is the active man—
even the industrialist. The world, for Heidegger (as for the Pragmatist) is a collection of tools; only for him (unlike the Pragmatist)
every tool inevitably turns against and frustrates the tool-maker.
There is much truth in this; but Heidegger takes no account of the
virtues bred by mutual help. His " authentic living " is without
reference to human relationships; and was found to be quite com-
patible with submission to Hitler.*

*Heidegger's philosophy, none the less, gives us back the sense of the
brittleness of both life and logic. For the linguistic analysts, this
whole discussion is meaningless; but most men know that Nothing
can mean something positive, as Night means something more than
Not-Day—words, like things, receive their colouring from the
viewpoint. Sartre has objected, in answer to Heidegger, that Death
cannot be man's " project " or " anticipation "—it comes unexpec-
tedly, and we know nothing really about it. This is no doubt true,
but it makes Death the more grandiose—not (as Sartre thinks) the
less; man is more than the beast because he can live, with full awareness, in uncertainty.*

*Heidegger's later philosophy is a confession of such uncertainty;
our notions of Death (since we are alive) hide the mystery from us—
we can know truth only as changing myth. God, in a sense, returns
to Heidegger—curiously, the Hegelian God who is History.
Heidegger turns from his unfinished Being and Time to the poetry
of Hölderlin. We can sympathise; but he was perhaps happier on
his bleak mountain-tops than in his attempts to soar. In his discovery
of the Transcendent he seems to have forgotten the Timor Mortis.*

I I

HEIDEGGER

THE SHUDDER BEFORE DEATH

FOR almost seventy years Kierkegaard slept; or, it might be truer to say, his voice could not rouse the world from its happy dream of Progress. The age, when it heard of him, reciprocated the dislike he felt for it; and though assured by Georg Brandes that he was a monument of Danish prose, it felt nothing was less urgent than to translate the monument. In his native Denmark itself, the ominous *prénom* " Soeren " came to be avoided at christenings. It was generally forgotten that Protestantism was, historically, a sombre creed; and the Reformation was looked on as the dawn of a rational humanism. The obstinate notion of the Fall, in all its forms, was a skeleton at the feast of Reason— a highly unwelcome mouse under the table-cloth. Only some German anti-clericalists, delighted by Kierkegaard's assaults upon the Lutheran Church, paid him a certain misconceived admiration. No one could have dreamed that the uncomfortable Dane would return in power from his unquiet grave.

In that dream of Progress, when all is said, there was much that we can applaud; it had the virtue and the danger of a myth—and not merely in the subjective sense of an illusion. It is a fault of most modern movements—from Marxism to Existentialism—to regard a " myth " as a useful fiction: whereas all myths are, of course, dangerous (though potent) in so far as they are fictitious, valuable in the degree that they contain truth. If hope can sometimes " create from its own

human-reality ex-sists as a self, that it can refer *itself* to the existent which has first of all to be transcended. In spite of being in the midst of the existent and surrounded by it, the human-reality, inasmuch as it is existence, has henceforth and forever transcended Nature. But that which happens to be transcended every time as existent in a human-reality was not at all just simply assembled there.[1]

And so on, through innumerable pages. In the whole production of Heidegger you will rarely find an image, a homely phrase, a concrete term; and the abstract terms are limited to a few dozen (almost all interchangeable and often bewilderingly interchanged[2]), recurring with sickening monotony like wooden horses in a merry-go-round. If the Absolute could speak, one feels, this might well be its language. Over the entire glacial surface of Heidegger's work there is no relief for the eye, no handrail, no foothold; this might be the philosophical equivalent of Scott's Last

[1] *Vom Wesen des Grundes.*

[2] For instance: there is no consistency in Heidegger's use of the term *das Seiendes*, which he equates usually with *Vorhandensein* or brute-reality, but occasionally also with *Dasein* or human-reality. (In the former sense it is sometimes called, for the sake of distinction, *das nicht daseinsmässige Seiende.*) *Dasein*, however, means at one time an individual self, at another is employed as synonymous with selfhood in general, and even, at yet another, as one property (among others) of the self. In his later essays it almost means " history ", and begins to look a little like the German nation! Again, *das Sein* is identified now with *das Seiendes* (in the sense of brute-reality), now with *Wesen* (essence); while in *Was ist Metaphysik?* a new term rears its head, *die Seiendheit* (is-ness). On occasion *Essenz* replaces *Wesen*, for reasons that are unclear. At the same time we are told, " The essence of being (*Dasein*) lies in its *Existenz*". *Existenz*, in Heidegger, is generally equivalent with *Transzendenz*, or— if you prefer it—*Sich-vorweg-schon-sein-in-der-Welt*. (In Heidegger's later works, *Existenz* turns into *Ek-sistenz*.) As for *Transzendenz*, Jean Wahl has noted four separate and incompatible meanings for that term in *Sein und Zeit*. None of these, of course, has anything to do with the traditional acceptation of " transcendence "—any more than *Existenz* is the scholastic *existentia* (Heidegger's *Vorhandensein*). It will be observed that, amidst all these terms, no real break is effected in the circle of a single idea—call it Being or call it Nothing (*das Nichts*).

Post in the Antarctic. Only a mollusc—or a professor—could project himself through these wastes, or nourish himself on such aliment.

Still, of course, Heidegger means something. For the student who has a seabird-like skill in grazing, skimming and swiftly snapping, this work has its own consistency and flavour: it is the actual flavour of Nothingness! Again like the Antarctic expedition, it is an attempt, not without its own grandeur, to chart the uttermost reaches: to bring the very edge and essence of Being within the compass of the mental traveller. In this sense, Heidegger is indeed the last of the great explorers in the history of thought—not its Columbus or its Livingstone but its Captain Scott; an explorer in an age when metaphysics, though still heroic, has come near to mere record-breaking and Press-sensationalism. The unfinished and unfinishable *Sein und Zeit* puts the full stop, or rather the question-mark, after the story of philosophy. The very prose—at once niggling and massive, like a needle manipulated by a giant—conveys, as perhaps nothing else could do, the sheer reality of Death.

. . . . . .

Heidegger, like Sartre, commenced as a pupil of Husserl—a " philosopher's philosopher " who, almost by an accident, gave the introspectionists a technique. To understand Heidegger's debt to Husserl, we must make something of a digression; for no two thinkers could well, in appearance, contrast more strongly. Husserl was a mathematician by training, who, though far removed from our logical positivists, felt a similar housemaidly zeal to clear philosophy of cobwebs. In the hope of making philosophy a true science of the psyche, Husserl criticised both philosophical idealism with its *a priori* categories and scientific materialism with its inductive methods. The Self was not just an object in the world, nor was the world a mere thought within a

Self, but the Self meant the consciousness, and consciousness was always consciousness of a world: the world was its necessary form and outward limit (in his language, its noematic co-relative). It was not (as Berkeley had said) that " to be is to be perceived ", but the perceiver in passing from one facet to another of the " perceived " gave it, as it were, its dimension of depth and significance. The act of consciousness was necessarily an " intention " towards an object: even feelings and moods (the " horizon of the co-intended ") were in that sense *objects* of experience. Consciousness was necessarily the consciousness of a consciousness—whether a perception or an emotion: an idea which has led, unfortunately, to all the jingles and rigmaroles so much beloved by the Existentialists. Neither was this idealism in the usual sense. Husserl (the Husserl, at least, of the early *Logische Untersuchungen*) admitted no super-individual transcendental subject; our different " significations " cross and interpenetrate. He did not deny that the outer world enjoys a sort of existence in its own right; he " bracketed " the question by a suspense of judgment in the manner of Descartes. A thing, for Husserl, was essentially a phenomenon or appearance (or rather, set of appearances) —though not in the Kantian sense that I construct it inside my own head; consciousness was a mere reference or pointer, like the shaft of light which pricks out form and colour. Thus I constitute a tree by walking round the tree— collecting the series of its aspects like a series of snapshots; but equally, by a sort of astronomical relativism, the tree which I circumambulate constitutes *me*, who *am* my movement round the tree. Husserl in effect[1] eliminated, at a single stroke, both the inaccessible Thing-in-itself and the

[1] The qualification is important. As we have seen, Husserl " bracketed " the question of Things-in-themselves, and he was not consistent in his theory of the Ego. In his later work (which happens to be better known in England) he restored the transcendental subject in full panoply.

independent Ego; he did not say that " Matter " was an illusion or that I generate the Cosmos out of thought, but I and the Cosmos made no sense apart from one another. One might almost say that if God died with Nietzsche, the Absolute became relativised with Husserl. The Husserlian terminology was peculiar, but this, I think, is a fair translation. Husserl himself, a logician of the hard school, scarcely anticipated what would be the consequences of his " phenomenology ".

The feeling one gets from Husserl's philosophy is one of " living on the edge "—of consciousness as a tightrope, stretched across a gulf; and Heidegger, who was no logician but very much of a poet, was quick to sense it. In Heidegger's attempted " ontology " Husserl's double-facing truth merged with Kierkegaard's despairing faith: on what was conceived as an economical *schema* for classifying " ideas " (a sort of Occamite razor-edge) the ghost of the romantic Dane stepped out and walked, like Hamlet's father on the battlements of Elsinore. Kierkegaard and Husserl,[1] who, if they could have met, would assuredly have had little to say to each other, are the progenitors of modern Existentialism, that strange amalgam of tough-minded naturalism and cosmic yearnings.[2] Its critics argue that it is just a new Idealism, in view of its summary way with objective nature

[1] One sees the affinity between Husserl's rope-ladders of relativism and Kierkegaard's abysses of separation from God. Take the following Kierkegaardian aphorisms: " A second belief is needed in relation to belief—the belief that one believes. Yes, one surely needs an extraordinary dose of belief to believe that a man believes—he himself has need of an extraordinary dose of belief to believe that he believes ".—*Journals.* Consciousness of sin "is the new sin of despairing of one's sin ".—*Sickness unto Death.* " The self is a relation to itself. . . . The self is not the relation, but the return of the relation upon itself."—*Sickness Unto Death.* Finally he cries in desperation, " The hardest thing fundamentally is to set a limit to the dialecticism of our unhappy relation to God ".—*Journals.*

[2] " When scepticism combines with longing, mysticism arises."—NIETZSCHE.

(the ungraciously named " brute-reality ") ; but the Existentialists claim, on the contrary, to have forced an issue out of
Idealism—through their insistence on danger, dread and
despair. By Husserl's *intention*, reappearing as Heidegger's
projection, they have as it were put together two " Nothings "
(namely " Selfness " and " Otherness ") and out of the impact
produced " Being ". Both the criticism and the answer,
perhaps, have their truth; I hold, as I have said, that
Existentialism has cracked the looking-glass of Idealism,
but has not yet opened a window on the world. It has
rediscovered tension, and thus given back to philosophy the
feeling of *architecture*, which merely abstract (so to say,
musical) philosophies have lacked; but it is so far only a
" functional " architecture. The religious wing of Existentialism—Buber, Marcel, Jaspers—speak to us of a communion
of souls, the mystical awareness of the " Thou "; but they
do not avoid using traditional moral concepts which fall a
little flatly on modern ears. There seems more hope in the
natural mysticism of the poets, to which Heidegger in his
old age (only a little over-loftily) points—Heidegger as the
Hölderlinist, a rather unhappy Moses on a solitary Pisgah,
with his rubrics broken and abandoned.

Idealism, the doctrine brought to completion by Hegel
upon the bases laid by the Renaissance philosophers, is
really an aristocratic philosophy, a sort of intellectual
landscape-gardening, proper to men who regard the Cosmos
as a *scene*—an extension of their enchanting personalities.
For Idealism, even the course of history (we have seen) is
something fixed and rounded off, like a play. The actors
are mere instruments of the authors and producers, who are
themselves the servants of the noble patrons and beholders:
action is a mere incident in civilisation, which in turn exists
for the contemplating Mind. This, I have suggested, is the
right and happy relationship, though it tends always (like
all happy things) to complacency, and in the ultimate

extreme to solipsism: for it reduces action and historical change to subordinate roles, which they will never permanently accept. Above all, Idealism is a *visual* philosophy; it is concerned only with the world that I clearly *perceive*. It knows nothing of that *other side* of reality which comes to life in the dark, when things and persons become independent foci of matter and energy—mere possibilities, capable of the most diverse realisations. Accordingly, all those philosophers who, in the nineteenth and early twentieth centuries, succeeded to the Great Tradition have gone in the opposite direction: in their various ways, they have tended to stress motion and the changing complex of relations—amidst which the independence of the Mind has been all but obliterated. They have sought, under the pressure of science and social reorganisation, to assimilate the Self to Processes. They are concerned, not with man the sovereign world-contemplator, but with man the time-traveller (Bergsonism), man the engine-driver (Pragmatism), man-in-a-railway-breakdown (Existentialism). Their emphasis is democratic: they accentuate the heat and strife of generalised activity, the common situation. It has been left to literature to champion the deposed Lord of Creation, now appearing as the " small man ", pathetic and frustrated—still dimly conscious of the world as the great Play, but now as a play " played upon him ", which he is forced to sit through or suffer in bewilderment. The Hegelian dialectic has become a bed of discomfort on which he is stretched. He may still guess, like Kafka, that his torments have a Meaning and Pattern; or, like Joyce, he may ironically attribute to them Patterns and Meanings, derived from theology or mythology, in which he scarcely believes at all. But it is this literature, and not the modern philosophies, which are on the side of Man. Only in Existentialism (in which orderly Process has returned to Chaos) does the individual recover a dazed independence and an almost heroic air. He is still a little man in a crowd, but the others (like fellow-passengers in a railway smash) are foreign bodies—some of them dead, some dangerously threatening, some possibly helpful and comradely, but all of them problematical. This is Pragmatism and Materialism —but with a difference: for the Self is again the centre. It is Idealism, if you will, but in reduced circumstances: for the limiting Non-Self—the unsought, quite senseless, *situation* into which Man is *thrown*—has become almost stronger than Man.

Husserl, however, was no Existentialist; and he regarded the vagaries of his pupil Heidegger without benevolence. He relegated him, indeed, to the class of the " psychologists "— in which he lumped metaphysicians and empiricists alike.[1] All that Husserl had meant to suggest was that in perceiving I perceive something, in thinking I think something, in feeling I feel something—even if it be only my own feeling: to be conscious, for human beings, was to be self-conscious. By this simplification he thought he had settled that tiresome " problem of knowledge " once for all. He did not affirm, like Kant, that things in themselves were inaccessible, but only partially inaccessible—since we apprehend them under aspects which can never be exhaustive; all experience is " infected " with chance and contingency. He therefore " bracketed " the whole question of existence; and this putting in brackets (the famous Husserlian *ēpochē* or "reduc- tion ") was advanced as a method, not a dogma.[2] His concern was not with existences but with *essences*: the basic " structures " (almost like Platonic ideas) of which experience

[1] Sartre, be it noted, is anathematised in similar terms by Heidegger. The word " psychology ", like the word " bourgeois ", gets a bad Press in these days—when every philosophy is psychological, and when all classes are indistinguishably " bourgeois ".

[2] Kierkegaard, one reflects, might have given Husserl an ironical approval. It was the former's contention that " in order to think existence at all, systematic thought must think it as abrogated, and hence as not existing "—*Concluding Unscientific Postscript.*

is composed. His watchword, as of a Bacon wearied with scholastic disputations, was " Back to the Facts " (under which term he included feelings and imaginations); and he was content to postpone the problem of whether a fact was in fact a fact. Heidegger was very little concerned with the analysis of appearance[1]; but he perceived the poetic or pathetic, as opposed to the practical, aspects of the Husserlite scheme. Deeply influenced by Kierkegaard (and by the circumstances of his time and nation) he saw Husserl's " intentionality " as a tragic leap: the desperate, perpetually renewed and useless effort by which Man seeks to transcend his nothingness.

" Intentionality " became " transcendence " and " project "; and these concepts were identified with *Time*, almost in the sense of Bergson's *Durée*.[2] Man throws Time before him, as if by a sort of Indian rope-trick. His existence is a being-in-anticipation; he is a bundle of possibilities out of which he must seek and choose the " greatest ", under pain of living the mere " unauthentic " existence of the crowd (which Kierkegaard had called simply " untruth "). And even the greatest of his possibilities is overshadowed and nullified by a greater the " possibility of impossibility ", namely Death. Why he " must " (or why he so often fails to do anything of the kind) is obscure, as Kierkegaard had left obscure how the divine command came

---

[1] *Sein und Zeit* is called by Heidegger an " ontology " by way of emphasising that it is not—like most modern philosophies—a logic or epistemology. It may be objected, however, that the first implies the second; Heidegger's edifice seems to be suspended in empty air. The alternative to the theoretic method is the poetic or " mystical " one, to which Heidegger goes over—with almost too much of a sweep of his gown—in his later work. But such a method must resign " ontological " ambitions. It must be, as Heidegger defines the essence of language, a *dialogue*—whereas the Classical system is a monologue.

[2] Heidegger, however, seems to be not much aware of Bergson, and his theory of Time (putting Death in the centre) seems to me an improvement on the French philosopher's.

to Abraham. The whole question, in short, of freedom and necessity is very inadequately treated by Heidegger, whose language (in spite of its air of pedantic precision) is emotional and evocative, and rendered still more obscure by his habit of treating the *Dasein* en bloc, as a single Person. This side of Existentialism was to be developed, but not notably clarified, by Sartre. Nor does Heidegger, or Sartre either, tell us by what measure some choices are " greater ", or more " authentic ", than others. This is the point most commonly made against Existential ethics. There is, I think, an answer to the objection, but the Existentialists have scarcely given the answer. Their omission to propose criteria can be defended on the same lines as the saying of Shaw, " The golden rule is that there is no golden rule ". Choices should vary in harmony with the ever-varying situation, and the sense for *the situation* pertains really to the æsthetic rather than to the moral faculty. However that may be, and I believe the Existentialists are here on an important track, the fact remains that they give a remarkably poor account of the matter. Almost invariably they speak, in the manner of Kierkegaard himself, as if the mere intensity or " pathos " of a choice made it a right one— though (unless they are Christians) they have none of Kierkegaard's Lutheran dogmatic justification.

Heidegger has often rebutted, not without warmth, the charge that his philosophy is " Idealist " [1]; and the charge is really unintelligent. He is in truth something quite different —to wit, a nihilist. Armed with the logical crowbar of Husserl's reduction, and the emotional blow-pipe of Kierkegaard's desperation, he has forced the door of Nothingness. He has " bracketed " Kierkegaard's after-life,

---

[1] Some critics, on the other hand, interpret Heidegger as a Scholastic " realist "; and it is true that one is constantly made aware of his Scholastic training, as in Sartre one feels the Cartesian background. In Heidegger's interpretation of Kant he really medievalises Kant.

and made extinction the reality of human existence. He has protested that for him Man and World cannot be separated, even in thought; but he has in fact united them like wrestlers in a death grapple. He has tidied up the loose ends of Kierkegaard, and turned the mathematics of Husserl to a sort of music; hence the ghostly symmetry, the real tragic beauty, of his system. With his achievement one can say, in the words of Thomson's *City of Dreadful Night*, " Here Hope died, starved out in its utmost lair ". Nevertheless he is in a sense a more refreshing fellow than the dreary prophets of Progress and Evolution. He does not turn the Individual (like Bergson) into an eddy in a whirlpool of Force, or (like Marx) into a screw twisted by Economic Determinism. He brings no flattering unction to self-deceiving utopianism; he half restores man to his grandeur— even though it be the *grandeur* of *misère*. It is significant, indeed, that the optimistic word *Becoming*, which Hegelianism made fashionable, is avoided by him. For him, there is no " synthesis " of Being and Nothing, and consequently (in spite of his later cult of history) no real historic change. Heidegger's system is as essentially static and anti-historical as Schopenhauer's—which is what gives it, like the latter's, its peculiar æsthetic appeal; for an issueless crisis, though an unpleasant rarity in life, can make extremely good art. Heidegger's world is like a still pool, on which the countless bubbles of *Dasein* rise and burst; of *das Seiendes*—the watery substance of the pool—we can know nothing, but though reduced to a mere film, it is in a sense the only reality.[1] This is the Leibnizian monad-system, but activated within by the expanding force of Nothingness—not prearranged

---

[1] In the later, more mystical, Heidegger the emphasis is shifted from the bubble to the pool—from the *Dasein* to the *Seiendes*, the latter appearing as " the Earthy " (*das Chtonische*). Here the word *Becoming* is first used: the æsthetic activity is called " the Becoming of Truth " (*das Geschehen der Wahrheit*).

by any presiding Harmony: symbol of the age, not of atomism, but of the atom bomb.

Heidegger, I have said, gives no " sufficient reason " for man's predicament, or his struggles; and this, in the last resort, invalidates his claim to be called an " ontologist ". Like all philosophers of Existence, he cannot really, as the Classical thinkers attempted to do, look at existence from the outside. Nevertheless he makes a brave attempt—so masterly, in fact, that it looks a little like cheating; for, as he holds (or did this insight only come latterly?) the whole progressive discovery of Truth since the pre-Socratics has been, at the same time, a " re-veiling " of it, and there is no escape from Error.[1] There is, in fact, a God or Dæmon in his system, and his name is Care (*Sorge*). It is Care, as man's preoccupation (*Besorgen*), which creates the World— Care which tempts him to hide and lose himself in it—Care which (in the case of a few) tears away his defences and reveals to him his " greatest possibility ", namely Death. Death, because it ends all, devalues all; for Heidegger as for Eastern mysticism (but without Nirvana), the creation is *guilt* (*Schuld*).[2] Yet by a tortured dialectic, derived from Hegel with improvements by Kierkegaard, man attains to " authentic living " by accepting and embracing his guilt. Repentance is naturally not here in question; but neither

[1] Heidegger might well have shown a connection (but has nowhere done so to my knowledge) between the vigour, whether successful or not, of Europe's philosophic effort, and the Platonic-Christian concentration on Death.

[2] Heidegger plays on the ambiguity of the German *Schuld*—which has of course the double meaning of guilt and debt. By my very being I cause a lack, or constitute a " negativity ", in some other being. " Guilt (*Schuldigsein*) does not first arise out of a (de)fault (*Verschuldung*), but the other way round: the latter is made possible only by a primordial Guilt."—*Sein und Zeit*. Heidegger employs the phrase " original Guilt ", but this is simply an instance of his confusing use of traditional Christian language. (Thus the sense of Guilt is conveyed by a silent " Call ".) The human reality, in fact, *is* Guilt—as it is *the foundation of negativity*.

74

is the feeling (for the sensitive, inseparable from life) of corporate responsibility for human evil. For Heidegger, in this more Nietzschean than Kierkegaardian, there is, it would seem, but one virtue: namely undaunted fatalism, the clear and courageous anticipation of Death—an anticipation, be it noted, which is often found in an exemplary degree among gangsters and murderers. It is this that distinguishes *men* from the mere " *man* " (the impersonal " one ")—the anonymous herd, who marry and give in marriage, eat, drink, and are merry when they can be. " *Das Man* " of course comprises, and will always comprise, the vast majority—for whom Heidegger, like so many German thinkers, expresses extreme contempt. They rarely, if ever, think of Death—wretched shirkers, unready to die, an ungallant band.[1]

Heidegger's system, like a draught of some strong opiate, has an overpowering effect, which makes it exceedingly hard to separate what is true in it from what is false. On account of its extreme formalism, it is difficult to relate it to one's experience; even the Self is rarely mentioned, its place being taken by the ghost-like *Dasein* (which indeed is scarcely a Self). Readers will swallow or reject such a metaphysic according to temperament; and most non-Germans, I should imagine, will hasten to pour it into the sink. And this is a pity, for Heidegger has really something valuable to say. It is true he has not shown us at all how the sense of Death enriches the quality of Life; and we are not much helped by such descriptions of it as " the possibility of impossibility ". Nor does there seem any sense, for a sceptic like Heidegger, in calling it " man's greatest possibility ";

---

[1] " The *one* cannot tolerate the courage capable of anguish in the face of death."—*Sein und Zeit*. It might be said that the " one " gives the courage necessary to overcome such anguish—whether or not this courage is always to be admired. Physical courage, though a virtue, is a gregarious virtue.

he is surely here stealing Christian overtones from Kierkegaard. The criticism of Sartre that Death is simply a
contingent fact, belonging to one's " facticity ", is sound so
far as it goes. Certainly a brooding on Death, like a brooding
on sexual desire, can easily become mere " morose delectation ". Yet, must we not admit that both Sex and Death,
the two great Irrationals, have been skirted around all too
gingerly by the old philosophies—whether sublimated by
religious decorum or cheapened by hygienic rationalism?
There is surely a sense, as Blake and Lawrence insisted, in
which a man is not alive in whom the senses do not *glow*;
and there is also a sense, as Heidegger and many German
poets make us feel, in which he is a corpse if he cannot
shiver.[1] And Heidegger is probably right in suggesting that
anxiety—the typical modern phenomenon called *worry*—is
rooted in fear of Death, fear which can be conquered only
by being realised and brought to consciousness. Even for
the atheist (perhaps one might say especially for him)
Death has its grandeur—but a grandeur which illumines and
aggrandises Existence. Surely Heidegger makes the mistake
of the gloomier sort of preacher, in arguing that Death
devalues Life—seeing that it gives it an edge and shape; the
very contrary is the truth, as indeed would seem to be
implied by his phrase " authentic living ". But as no man
in his senses ever doubted that he would die, Heidegger's
scorn for the Crowd seems too unqualified. In confronting
his end, the most slavish mortal is an Individual.[2]

Heidegger, it is true, has in a sense anticipated the latter
objection; he suggests that all men deep in their hearts (all,
that is, except the courageous clear-sighted few) nourish the

[1] Heidegger insists, quite rightly, on the uncanniness (*Unheimlichkeit*)
of the world, as revealed to him who lives in the authentic mode. One
recalls Pascal's fright before the eternal spaces.

[2] Heidegger himself, in fact, admits this and says it better in the
aphorism. " Every man is born as many men and dies as a single one ".

hope that they will be exceptions, that they will live forever on the earth or, at least, survive beyond the usual span. Everyone, so to say, believes obstinately in some Elixir of Life, as all bald men hope for the perfect hair-restorer. The famous syllogism " All men are mortal, Socrates is a man, therefore Socrates is a mortal " starts, after all, from an unreasoned " major ", as logicians love to demonstrate. The notion of a new " mutation ", presented by a hundred ingenious theorists from the Count de Cagliostro to Gerald Heard, is the oldest dream of humanity. All this is perhaps true; and it might be an excellent thing, as in the case of the dread of Death, if we were to present it clearly to our consciousness and draw the consequences. If we were to live forever (or even twice the normal span) what should we do? Would the bore continue prosing, and the sayer of smart things continue uttering smart things? Would the business man and the politician persist unwearyingly in their squalid manœuvres? Would everything be the same, only more so— as in Sartre's excellent film-fantasia, *Les Jeux sont Faits*, in which a pair of lovers, dying frustrated, are given a " second chance "? Personally I see no reason to doubt it; there is nothing so seductive as habit and routine. In the end (to continue the fancy) life itself would atrophy; the civil servant going to his office might become a real automaton—driven by a momentum accumulated through the æons! In short (and apart from such dubious possibilities) it is *endlessness*, not Death, which devalues Life. And this is not simply an illusion due to scale, for existence would really, in such an event, be deflated—our " projects " lose all vital force. Heidegger, the Hellenist, seems more medieval than truly Grecian in his pessimism: he has missed the *double* sense of the saying that " those whom the Gods love die young ".

In a way, Heidegger does understand this; for it is his main merit to have stressed, more than any man, the constant interdependence of Death and Life. But he has given his

77

insight an unnecessarily sombre tinge—unworthy of philosophy, which should be a joyful wisdom. The " moral " of his demonstration, like Schopenhauer's, is really suicide; and though both the great pessimists condemn this course, their counter-arguments do not seem remarkably deterrent. Moreover Heidegger (the Heidegger of *Sein und Zeit*) knows nothing of those moments when we are, as one poet has phrased it, " at leisure from ourselves ", and as little concerned with " Life " as Death. Death, as we have seen, is the " Prime Mover " in his Cosmos—the invisible peak in the rope-trick by which the *Dasein* creates Time and World (by which, in his language, it " worlds "). But apart from this metaphysical undertone, the system is uncompromisingly pragmatist, and anything but quietistic or life-denying. It has been compared in fact with that of the inoffensive Mr. Dewey. Heidegger exhibits the very German combination of a fascination for *Technik* and a lust for tragedy; he is one half Eastern Yogi and the other half an American " prospector " (or, to keep to his terms, a projector). One might call him in fact a *pessimistic pragmatist* (that rather unusual thing); he is too sceptical of " pure reason " to conduct a search—like Kant—into the foundations of metaphysics, and he is too much of a tragic poet to be content with the prosaic assumptions of pragmatism. The term *Dasein* (or mere " being-there ") seems indeed an unhappily chosen one for the Self, which, as he describes it, is as ceaselessly active as Bergson's *Elan Vital*, though in a private universe. The *Dasein* is not a Cartesian " substance " which perceives and cognises—it is a *possibility* which projects and discovers [1]; and " dis-covery ", for Heidegger, means a carving and fashioning of the raw " brute-reality ". Man confers

---

[1] There is, however, a sort of ghost of common-sense realism in the doctrine that the *Dasein* can fall into Untruth—just as the Crowd exists " unauthentically "; but Heidegger is careful to distinguish Untruth from simple Error (which, for him, could have no meaning).

78

meanings on things (which in themselves they wholly lack)[1] in accordance with his desires and practical interests—driven by the dæmon Care, in the double sense of Anxiety and Preoccupation.[2] And for Heidegger, as for all Pragmatists, thought and action are one; so far as thought pretends to be an independent activity, it is the villain of the piece. I do not *choose* my "possibility" by a process of thought or even comparison; I *am* my possibility. The *Dasein* finds itself obstructed, not by any intractability in the nature of things, but by that painful matter, its own Past: by the sum of realised and petrified "possibles". Like a spider it spins the web of Time and World, so to say, out of its bowels, casting a changing net of meanings over the "brute-reality"; only, by the curse of restlessness which has been mysteriously laid upon it, it must restitch the net at every instant, with the result that the lines become constantly tangled up. Or one might compare it to the animal in Kafka's very frightening tale, *The Burrow*—perpetually running hither and thither demolishing and repairing; for in proportion as he extends his cells and corridors, he chokes them with ever-accumulating rubble, and lays himself open to attack on a wider front. And as he delves and frets, one rumour (hardly to be distinguished from his heart-beats) is always in his ears, one image builds itself before his imagination: the sound and sight of the oncoming *larger* beast which will one day have him by the throat.[3]

This, it will be agreed, is an excellent picture of man in the twentieth century—and it is, I think, a very exact like-

[1] "All being which is not of the nature of the *Dasein* must be understood as senseless, as essentially altogether devoid of meaning." "Utility is the ontological-categoric definition of being as it is ' in itself '."—*Sein und Zeit*. The later Heidegger, however, seems to have departed from this position.

[2] Heidegger's discussion of psychological space and time is perhaps the part of *Sein und Zeit* which is most solid.

[3] Kafka's better-known work *The Trial* is almost equally Heideggerian.

ness of the Heideggerian *Dasein*; but considered as a symbol of man on the earth, it seems to leave out certain things. Works of art, for instance (among which one must count *Being and Time* and *The Burrow*)—though owing much of their inspiration to a sense of the brevity of life, if not to simple hunger—have in them, surely, the quality of *eternity*. They do not, unless we are impatient, stand in the way of fresh projects [1]; and they dispose the mind (if Heidegger will allow the term) to a feeling, finally, of calm. Human beings, moreover, have other moods than the active—even in the sense of the creative.[2] There is an evening of the day—an evening of life—one may even hope, by analogy, for an " evening ", a " Saturnian Age ", after the whole human effort—when they can sit back and enjoy: even if enjoyment be the keener for a spice of sadness. They can enjoy (what is more) not only the contemplation of their own works, but, as some have thought, the phenomena of non-human nature —and not value a river simply as a " natural frontier ", or a landscape for the crops and minerals which it may yield. All this is banal enough, and Heidegger—a learned humanist

[1] Heidegger, in spite of his considering the world as composed of tools, speaks little of *machine*-tools, and does not analyse their effects in blocking new projects (owing to the capital which has been sunk in them).

[2] In a sense, Heidegger believes less in Action than does Sartre; this is a consequence of his disdain for the Crowd, and his more traditional conception of the role of the philosopher. Although the world for him (as for Sartre) is a network of projects, the Crowd who are absorbed in these projects are yet living " unauthentically "—whereas *les salauds*, in the Sartrian system, mean simply the respectable people. The " world as world " is only revealed to me when things go wrong. If, for instance, I want to do some hammering and have lost the nails, I find that I see the hammer for the first time: not, however, as a pure form (as a Platonist might say), but as a portion of the original Nothingness. If I were to look at it for long enough, I would end by forgetting its purpose; it would lose its very essence and definition. This is something different from Sartre's active repulsion before brute Nature. In Sartre, Nature herself (the *En-Soi*) has really moved into the position of *das Man*. The later works of Heidegger, on the other hand, announce a sort of Dionysiac Nature-mysticism.

Martin Heidegger

who lives, like a romantic poet, in a hut of the Black Forest
—is not to be accused of philistinism. In one of his commen-
taries on Hölderlin, he in fact declaims—rather rhetorically
for an English taste—against our thinking of his " Swabian
sea ", the *Bodensee*, as a mere geographical or " commercial-
technical" section ("*Wie lange noch? Wie lange. . . ?* "). But
it is the strange fact that, among the few images employed
in *Sein und Zeit*, almost all are drawn from manufactured or
processed objects, scarcely any from the ancient world of
Nature.[1] Thinkers like Schopenhauer, possessed with a
nobler pessimism, have been troubled by the *cruelty* of Nature
—and there is a sense in which the sufferings of animals are
more pitiful than those of humanity; but Heidegger's world
is much too egocentric, or at least anthropocentric, for that.
For Heidegger it would seem (as for the Catholic theologian)
the brutes are *things*—created for human ends: accorded at
most the " being " (*das Seiendes*) of a participle.

Still, Heidegger's nihilism has a grain of wholesome truth.
The hoarded banknotes return to pulp, the anxious flesh to
muck—it has often been said, and will bear repetition. The
existence of Kafka's animal in *The Burrow* was really worth-
less—rendered so by the inevitability of his defeat; and the
allegory *seems* to fit large sectors of our life. Why then is
Heidegger's analysis (like the rather different analysis of
Schopenhauer) finally unacceptable, even as regards much
restless and futile human striving? I think it is because of
the disingenuous " Idealist " trick of slipping easily from the
Absolute to the individual Ego and back again, of " playing
upon the two tables ". The philosopher identifies himself,
and *must* identify himself, with the Unity behind Things—

---

[1] It can be replied that the same is true of Plato; but Plato's fascination by " artefacts " was not utilitarian. However, I believe it to be
true (as I argued in *The Twilight of the Ideas*) that the Platonic Forms had
something " machine-made " about them, and that it was the conception of the Idea as a mould or stamp which gave us—by a natural
development—the Machine.

(call it transcendental Subject, Idea or Being) and treats the multitudinous mundane reality as simply " Otherness "; but he has the right to do this only while he is thinking trans-cendentally—while he is speaking, if I may put it so, *ex cathedra*. His empirical self and the empirical *other selves* of which he writes remain exactly on the same plane—as indifferent compared with " Being " as, for the Christian, they are equal before God. The *I*, as Buber and Marcel rightly insist, implies the *Thou*, whereas beside the Absolute both I and Thou are in another dimension. Nor is the Absolute, except in metaphor, anything like a personal God —as philosophers such as Hegel and Heidegger, deeply rooted in Christianity, are apt to imagine or to imply. The Absolute is neither " I " nor " Thou ", neither God nor devil—it is a simple necessity of thought, like the Zero in arithmetic; the individual cannot incarnate the Absolute in any exclusive sense. And yet it is the tendency of Idealist thinkers (and Heidegger in this respect is among them) to write always as if the individual, whether man or larger unit, were alone in the world, and the others were—just the others. Hence the partly justified disrepute of Hegelianism, and the popularity of the Kierkegaardian revolt; but Kierkegaard, though to a lesser extent than Heidegger, is not at all free from the same taint. Kafka's animal in *The Burrow*, occupied with simple self-preservation, has nothing heroic; and neither—in reason—has Heidegger's " Being-in-the-World", at grips with Care. Human beings, however, are moved not merely to " project " and to " transcend ", but are also capable of meeting in their common " transcendence ". Even if group interests and aims be vain or senseless, there can be a place for high disinterestedness and fraternal feeling within the group. That there is really no place for either in the monistic philosophy of Heidegger is an impor-tant weakness. The same criticism also holds, as we shall see, for the semi-pluralistic scheme of Sartre, though it is belied (inconsistently, it is true, with his metaphysic) by his democratic faith.

It may be objected that, for Heidegger, persons no less than things are the objects of man's *Sorge* (called in this instance *Fürsorge* or " solicitude "); for the others are involved, at every moment, in my " projects ". Certainly he preaches no " Ivory Tower " æstheticism. Not for a single instant can man separate himself—even in solitude—from the total situation (the *Mitsein*); we have seen that, for Heidegger, there is no distinct " thinking substance " or subject such as we find in Descartes or in Kant. But this dependence is merely a part of the *Dasein's* " Fall "—by which is meant the calamity of existence, as in most Eastern thought; and though there is perhaps a sense and a mood in which this is true, it is to be observed that the " authentic living " is not conceived as deepening or transforming human relationships.[1] How could it, when the only authentic experience is the essentially individual one of dying: not art-creation, nor communal work, nor even communal revolt? Yet we cannot admit that there is anything " unauthentic " about what Whitman called " the love of comrades "—which has redeemed, often enough, even the violence and verbiage of trade union politics. For the many martyrs of the working-class and other movements, Death was indeed their " greatest possibility ", though not always their greatest " anguish ": a feeling at times powerfully conveyed even in the turbid, tortured novels of Malraux. The only value for Heidegger is Death—one's own death (which, he says, reveals the totality of the World as World): so that *the others* are finally an obstruction, as was Regine for Kierkegaard. And this goes much farther than did the

[1] It is true that Heidegger admits an " authentic " *Mitsein*. But this means only that I can relate the Others to my own supreme project, to wit, my death. One has to note also that the " solicitude ", and the " consideration " (*Rücksicht*) that goes with it, turn out to mean merely awareness, and may cover every form of enmity.

great Gautama, or even Schopenhauer—thinkers who preached Liberation through Pity. It is a matter on which one does not like to dwell, but Heidegger's acceptance of Nazism is a sorry commentary on his rather lofty disdain for " the Crowd "; the extremest expression of the Mob-spirit in all history found in him an obedient—though not entirely willing—servant.[1] The picture of this fine thinker preaching submission to Hitler, and reading the commemoration address on the wretched Schlageter, is one from which we can only turn in shame and disgust. No philosopher ever aimed higher or ventured farther in his thought than Heidegger; no philosopher, in his public attitudes, has—at certain moments—sunk so low.

· · · · ·

The great achievement of Heidegger, I have suggested, is to have restored the backcloth of Nothingness to the Mind— even if his prose seems, perhaps inevitably, to be over-weighted with those sable curtains.[2] He makes us, like no other philosopher, feel *Nothing* as palpable, corporeal, active

[1] This must be said with one important reserve. Though Heidegger could write " Only the Führer himself is the German Reality, present and past, and its law ", he at no time would have anything to do with " racism ". During his rectorship of Marburg University, he refused to allow the names of Jews like Husserl and Bergson to be struck off the course.

[2] Such words as the following (from *Was ist Metaphysik?*) have an undeniable power:

" It is only because the Nothing is revealed to us in the very foundation of our human-reality that the utter strangeness of the existent can assail us. It is only on the condition that its strangeness oppresses us that the existent can awaken and compel our wonder. It is only by reason of the wonder—that is to say, through the manifestation of the Nothing—that there arises the ' Why? ' It is only because the ' Why ' is possible as such, that we can in a definite fashion question and prove. It is only because we can question and prove, that the destiny of the *explorer* is given into our charge."

One is reminded of the fine line of Novalis, *Du bist der Tod, und machst uns erst gesund.*

(" the Nothing *nihilates* ")[1]: and surely, notwithstanding the paradox, with reason, for *wanting* and not *having* is the dynamic of existence—the active principle of time and change is the negative principle and not the positive. Heidegger's Nothing is not the negative of logic—even of Hegel's logic[2]; it is " before " Being. In different words, it is the sense of infinity, which makes us feel (if we are truly alive) our finitude and fragility. Lacking that quasi-sensual feeling for the Dark, we have lost, almost, the intellectual apprehension of the Light: our philosophy has come near to being —like that of the late medieval schools—mere verbalism and logic-chopping, with a realist-idealist debate in place of the realist-nominalist one. A corpse is a difficult thing to fit into a philosophy! It is not a Subject, it is not in the ordinary sense an Object, it is neither Self nor Not-Self; it upsets every category, like Poe's ghostly dancer spreading confusion in the ballroom. It is like a mirror-image, and in a sense it is one: the reflexion I see when I look into the future. In a universe without Death (if such a thing can be imagined) we should be mere solipsists; we would never really believe in a " world outside ". Time has been called many things, but it is foremost of all a flight from our own graves.

These truths, perhaps, are not altogether new ones,[3] but they have never been more powerfully suggested than by Heidegger; his work seems like a Baroque catafalque of prose. Doubtless to the logical positivist this whole discussion is—in the most banal sense—a fuss about nothing. Even if

[1] " *Der Tod wird gross und hat einen eigenen Wert.*"—F. Marnau.

[2] Heidegger's saying *das Nichts nichtet* is not to be understood as a Hegelian " negation of the negation ". In this respect, Sartre is closer than Heidegger to Hegel (*Le Néant est neantisé*). Heidegger's Nothing is felt almost as a spirit which drives man to create a world; for Sartre, " nihilation " is the actual mode of man's activity. In Heidegger's phrasing, man is an outpost (*Platzhalter*) of the Null; in the version of Sartre, man " secretes " Nonentity in the exercise of his freedom.

[3] It is nevertheless remarkable that almost every definition of Time, from Plato's to Bergson's, leaves out the essential reference to Death.

he admitted that Life and Death are any concern of philosophers, he would probably reply with the superficial adage of Epicurus, " If *we* exist, Death is not yet—if *it* exists, we are no longer there." To him, the remarks " I love Nothing ", " I fear Nothing ", can only mean " I do not love ", " I do not fear "; what fallacy more gross than to use Nothing as a name? (In strictness, " Night " for him should mean " Not day ", " Naughtiness " should be just " Not niceness " —for both words mean simply the *Not* or *Nought*; and if he would follow this trail he would soon find all the old questions still awaiting him.) It needs, however, a certain temerity to declare that words " can only mean "—this or that: especially such very problematic and equivocal words as " love ", " fear ", " Nothing " and even " I ". It may be suggested, in fact, that we are here in the realm of metaphysical questions (which is as much as to say, meta-logical ones). Every man of the smallest sensibility knows what is meant by saying " I love Nothing "—spelt with a capital N: it means something very close to saying " I love Everything ". It means that I love the element of negativeness or vacancy in things—still scenes, solitudes, empty spaces, " lost " hours of the day; it means that I feel almost, in the title words of a play by W. B. Yeats, that " Where there is Nothing there is God ", or as Sophocles' Œdipus said, "When I am nought, in that hour, I am a man ". Similarly, " I fear Nothing " means that the same conditions and states evoke my fear.[1] That most of the Existentialists seem to know

[1] Logical positivists are fond of quoting the professorial quips of *Alice in Wonderland* and *Through the Looking-Glass*: " What excellent eyes you must have! To be able to see Nobody—and at that distance! " etc. Those excellent books for Victorian children were naturally not designed to frighten. Adults, perhaps, may see humour, and something else as well, in such lines as these by George Macdonald:

" As I was going down the stair
I met a man who wasn't there;
He wasn't there again today—
I only wish he'd go away! "

little of the love and a great deal of the fear (or as they prefer to call it, the dread or *Angst*) is certainly a criticism of their systems; but there is a true sense in which the fear of Nothing, in philosophy, is the beginning of Wisdom.

M. Sartre, who has no sympathy for Nordic Death-nostalgias, has forcibly criticised Heidegger on two counts: namely for his description of Death as man's " anticipation ", and as his " project ". Man, he argues, can never *anticipate* Death, because all that he knows or will ever know about it is that he has seen other men die. Nor can Death be his *project*, seeing that it comes at its own time—proverbially like a thief in the night—defying even the nicest calculations of the actuaries. Even suicide is not properly a project, but only the evasion of all projects; it gains its significance, like all closed things, from the projects of others—the survivors. In short, Death is " absurd ", and its absurdity renders Life absurd. For Heidegger also, we have seen, Death takes the value out of Life, though the recognition of the fact (by a curious paradox) somehow gives Life back its value; but Sartre stops short of this particular dialectical twist. For him as for Heidegger, man's grandeur is in his hopeless Will; but the emphasis is shifted—insensibly but definitely—to the Will, and away from the Despair.

These criticisms of Sartre's are no doubt cogent; for Heidegger's style is always somewhat rhapsodical and imprecise. But their effect, it seems, to me, is to enhance the significance of Death. If Death were an event that could be arranged it would be, so to speak, no longer a temporal but a spatial term; to use Sartre's own illustration, it would be like the arrival in Paris of the train from Chartres. Until the last moments of our earthly journey, we should never experience Death " upon our pulses ". Safe within its invulnerable walls, our Life would lack—along with its danger—all real savour, and, as I have suggested, all sense of the outer world. It would resemble, in fact, the life of

that rather mythical entity, *das Man*. But we can answer
Sartre in his own language, for the question takes us into his
special " universe of discourse ", namely that of the ever-
lasting games of the Subject and the Object. For Sartre,
the peculiar nastiness of Death is that it makes of one's life a
Thing, like a natural object—a sealed-off and rounded
whole; a *plaything*, indeed, in the hands of others—by whom
he apparently means the gossips, biographers and historians.
There is, I myself should have supposed, something stimulat-
ing as well as frightening in this idea—the thought that I
carve my life like a statue; and no artist worthy of the name
is unduly troubled by a " bad Press ". However, be that as
it may; there is an older and really unfortunate sense in
which Death makes of a man an *object*—an object which, in
anticipation, he carries with him all his days. .Man is not
more than the beast because he dies, but because he knows,
and can live with the knowledge, that he is " fastened to a
dying animal ". A death artistically integrated into his
life, the " resolution of a melody "—even if it were possible—
would make him not greater but in fact something lesser
than he is. Li-Tai-Po may drown in clasping the moon's
reflexion, Rilke succumb gracefully to a rose-thorn—but
it is all in vain. It is perhaps cleaner and more genuine, as
Leo Chestov [1] said, to expire like a dog in a ditch than,

---

[1] Leo Chestov, one of the most brilliant and bizarre of the Existentialists, spent his life in attacking the Reason—by the aid of which men
seek (in vain) to shelter themselves from the unknowable and the
unpredictable, from uncertainty and dread. In this sense he criticised
Kierkegaard for remaining in the Ethical Stage. This criticism may
seem a contradiction of what we have said; but one understands
Chestov's meaning. Kierkegaard, after all, never got farther than an
evangelistic Protestantism—for the reason that he did not *really* (and
quite simply) believe in the Miraculous and the Supernatural. Chestov
goes so far as to suggest that if Kierkegaard had had faith he would have
recovered his virility (supposedly lacking), and that this was the
" Repetition " which he vainly hoped to achieve. " In this terrifying
experience was revealed to him what the majority of men do not even
suspect: that absence of faith is the expression of impotence, or that

even, like Socrates—discoursing, with forced calm, among his friends. In the words of J. M. Synge's *Deirdre*, " Death is a poor untidy thing though it's a queen that dies ".

.   .   .   .   .

Heidegger, then, is right in giving back to Death the importance (though of another kind) which it enjoyed in Christian philosophy, and of which it has been dispossessed in most post-Renaissance philosophies. It is Death, and not the *Elan Vital*, which creates Time—or which provides the necessary springboard for every *élan*. It is true that, by dropping not only Kierkegaard's God[1] but any possible " I and Thou " relationship, Heidegger unduly darkens the picture. Still, *Sein und Zeit* has zest, if not joy; it is in a sense of a more optimistic cast than the lectures and essays which have followed it. It is a voyage of discovery, while the latter suggest a rather dejected " homecoming ".[2] In these we hear almost nothing of Death and authentic Living—there is even some talk of " the Joyous " (*das Freudige*) and " joyous shuddering " (*Freudigschauern*). But in the main we are treated to a shifting shadow-play of the Overt (*das Offene*) and the Errant (*die Irre*), the Revealing (*Ent-bergen*) and the Re-veiling (*Ver-bergen*)—and *Eksistenz* has sprouted a twin called *In-sistenz* (which, curiously, replaces *das Verfallen*)[3]. One gets the impression that Heidegger has quite lost his bearings; and for a good reason. The Nothing has in fact

impotence witnesses to absence of faith."—*Vox Clamantis in Deserto.* Chestov died in Paris in 1939, alone and in deep poverty—very much like a dog in a ditch! (His disciple Benjamin Fondane—also of importance in the history of Existentialism—had an even starker ending, in the gas-chambers of the Nazis.)

[1] Some students, it is true, have understood the mystics' " super-essential One " by Heidegger's *Sein* within the *Seienden* (also called by him *das Es*, the " It ").

[2] The reference is to his commentary on Hölderlin's elegy *Heimkunft* (Homecoming).

[3] See particularly *Vom Wesen der Wahrheit* (1943).

nihilated the system, as it was bound to do; those deep wells could only be sunk at the cost of wrecking the foundations. Perhaps no one will ever attempt such a structure again; even Sartre's prodigious *L'Etre et le Néant* really breaks off half-way through, and turns into a sort of psychological observer's notebook. Heidegger had called Death the one Reality—the " clearing " (*Lichtung*) in the density of Being—in whose light is revealed to us " the World as World ": which was all very well, but in " anticipating " Death we are still alive. As Sartre objected, the Conscious cannot really anticipate Unconsciousness; and the world, to be made manifest, must be capable of manifestation. In short, if Being is by definition the Unknown (that is, for our minds, Nothing), every *revealing* of it must be a *re-veiling*. Heidegger attacks the Scholastic definition of Truth as the " adequation of the mind to the thing "; " Truth ", he says, " is not the mark of some correct proposition made by a human ' subject ' in respect of an ' object '." (Heidegger's language may seem woolly, but that is doubtless because his remark, if " correct ", cannot as we see be " true ".) And what can that mean but that no proposition can be true? Plato, he holds, began the whole trouble with his doctrine of Ideas; we cannot in fact leave this World-Cavern, so that, for us at least, the shadows are truer than the light.[1] *Das Man*, it would almost appear, was right after all: right because he is wrong, or only wrong because he appears to be right. The Humean scepticism would seem to be complete.

And yet it is not quite—for we can surely see emerging a pattern which is Hegelian: we were right in calling the old spell-binder the last philosopher, for Heidegger's fine bravura-display has failed.[2] Heidegger, in *Sein und Zeit*, saw the human effort as a " Fall "—a Fall from which man can

[1] See *Platons Lehre von der Wahrheit* (1942).
[2] Jaspers who preserves the religious accent of Kierkegaard, seems similarly to have ended as a sort of Hegelian historiographer.

raise himself by a vision of Death. Since then he has realised, apparently, that the latter was a mere phrase. Whatever Death is, it cannot be a vision; it is rather the limit of our visual field, beyond which begin (as religion, in its own manner, teaches) the things that can be *felt*, but never *known*. It must follow, however, that mere human vision is itself the " Fall ": the changing partial perspective of man's consciousness through the ages—to use a term of Heidegger's new vocabulary, man's " Counter-Essence " (*Gegenwesen*). *History*, and not Death, is now the God: a God who, at his pleasure, comes and goes. Heidegger, the ex-theological student, returns to a sort of piety: a man does not, any more, " transcend himself "—rather he " waits " for the Transcendent.

Nevertheless, it is Hegelianism with a difference. Borrowing a phrase from Hölderlin, Heidegger calls historical dialectic " conversation "—a new and hopeful word in his vocabulary! The most solitary of philosophers has discovered a kinship, across a century, with the loneliest of poets. He has found in Hölderlin the thinker, and a thinker for this age, somewhat as Mr. Middleton Murry has found a philosopher in Keats. After reducing the German language to a wilderness of hyphened particles[1], he has learnt that " the Word " was in the beginning, and that philosophy divorced from poetry must wither. For it is the poet who discovers " the gods "—the transcendent Essences—which for Heidegger means, as we have seen, that he creates them; though it would make equal Husserlite sense to say that the Essences create history and a world. The phenomenological theory of truth as a projection—in which "Something" is created, so to say, out of two " Nothings "—is true in fact of art, and only of art: little as Husserl perhaps cared about artists. (We find indeed a similar confusion between representation

---

[1] It is not for nothing that Heidegger's first published work was a treatise on the Subtle Doctor, Duns Scotus.

and expression in the once-fashionable æsthetic of Croce.)
The theory is true, that is to say, on certain deep levels, but
not true at all on the level where Husserl wished to apply it—
that of the individual self-consciousness. It is true of those
rare moments in which we seem able to " stand back "—not
only from the world but from our own consciousness, and in
which the world itself drops out of sight. Yet it is a theory
which has also a symbolic value at the present time, when the
artist has succeeded, in his turn, to the place of the priest
and the scientist as man's spiritual director. Nevertheless
Heidegger's latest essays give us a feeling, not any more of
bleakness, but rather of vacuousness—of a tepid diffuseness,
like the ultimate death by entropy of our Cosmos; the
hunting of the Infinite has ended in that astro-physical
twilight-sleep! Dr. Heidegger sits among the immortals—
himself a small, a very small, immortal—like one of the
fabled Himalayan sages, waiting for new Gods to be born out
of the pool of Nothingness. We share his hope; we too
believe that the myths are eternal, and that the Reality
behind the daily mediocrity is æsthetic. He seems, however,
to have lost sight of one small matter—one thing which he
of all men should have remembered—a thing by which more
sensitive, if less subtle, minds have been more than usually
troubled in the 1940s. He has forgotten, to all appearance,
that Men must die.

III

SYNOPSIS: SARTRE

Sartre is perhaps the greatest intellectual force today. But is he a " Force for Good "? Does he hate evil things because of their likeness to good ones? Sartre is a more sadistic Bernard Shaw. But he is also a metaphysician, with his roots in Jansenism; and he has infected the French with the troubled thought of Germany. Like all Jansenists, he has a fascinated sense of evil. Again like all Jansenists, he tends to identify evil with Nature. He cannot forgive the flesh for its suffering. With much humour—and a sort of poetry—he describes (in La Nausée) how the very trees in the park inspire repulsion. The aim of Man (the Pour-Soi), for Sartre, is the impossible one of becoming one-with-himself like an object in Nature (the En-Soi). But if Nature is disgusting, such an effort must be disgusting also— and that in fact is how Sartre makes us regard it. More disgusting still is the tendency of the Self to become an object in the sight of another person. The feeling that " one never knows who is looking " is, for Sartre, the refutation of solipsism. It is also, he holds, the origin of conscience. Thus the world becomes shattered into a myriad reflecting surfaces and distorting perspectives. This is an interesting application of Husserl-theory to psychological space, as it was applied by Heidegger to psychological time; but Sartre turns the idea to rather cheap melodramatic uses. Sartre sees every activity, bodily or mental, as an appropriation—alimentary or sexual; he is (so to say) a Freudian without the theory of the Unconscious, just as he is a Marxian without Economic Determinism. Sexual love itself is the supreme attempt to capture the Other—not however as a thing but as a freedom; and the instrument of such appropriation is the Eye. Human relationship, for Sartre, falls into five divisions—love, masochism, desire, sadism and (last but not least) hate; and Sartre shows, with a wealth of detail, why all five must fail. These analyses are, on the whole, more curious than helpful.

For all that, Sartre makes us feel—as no other philosopher—the mystery of the " Outside "; for if my Esse *is my* Percipi, *I have as many existences as there are perceivers. Only (true to his basic Jansenism) he sees the relation between Outer and Inner as one of frustration merely.*

Sartre irritates by his schoolboy jibing at religion; nevertheless, the attempt to find new bases for ethics in an age of agnosticism is important. Sartre is too much of a Jacobin to rest in Despair; his philosophy is really a reassertion of human Freedom. What does he mean by this ambiguous word? We should distinguish between moral *freedom (upheld in a manner by the medieval Church and denied by the Reformers) and* psychological *freedom (upheld in substance by the old " common sense " rationalism and denied by the post-Darwinians). Sartre, though an atheist, is really concerned with* moral *freedom; he talks the language (strange to Anglo-Saxon ears) of a medieval heresiarch. But, while affirming " responsibility ", he, in effect, makes man wholly irresponsible. When criticised on this score, Sartre produced a warmed-up mess of Socratic reason and Kantian moralism. Still, Sartre's emphasis on the individual evokes one's sympathy; but he goes farther, and drops into a sort of mystical solipsism. This is really a wilful confusion between the super-personal and the empirical Self. If I will myself and my world, where was the need for the Sartrian disgust? Why should not the contemplator's Eye, in seeing the world, also see that it is good? A man, after all, has* two *eyes; does not this fact suggest that the law of life is balance, and that opposites (as Hegel taught) can be reconciled in the " total view "? But Sartre, the impatient anarchist, shies away from this conclusion; his philosophy of freedom drops, quite naturally, into the " absurdism " of some of his contemporaries. For this, however, there is a certain justification in the present world-situation; every ideal and " ideology " seems either empty or suspiciously " totalitarian ". The Will today must be an expression of the whole personality, springing from the Unconscious; and here Sartre—with all his spiritual distempers—preaches the same doctrine as D. H. Lawrence. In his first novel he seemed even to be groping towards the " imaginative reason " of Coleridge and Blake; but the Occupation propelled him—and this was to his credit—towards Action. Since then, unfortunately, he can only conduct an aimless journalistic guerrilla-warfare. His promised Ethic takes the form of an amusing scatological work. His game of antinomies (which in* Being and Nothing *was more than a game) becomes a mere kaleidoscope, in which all things change their names, and nothing any longer means anything.*

Our final impression of Sartre is, however, nothing evil, but one of an exhilarating and courageous mind, which just misses being a great one.

Jean-Paul Sartre

III

SARTRE

THE SHUDDER BEFORE *THE OTHER PERSON*

JEAN-PAUL SARTRE is probably the greatest intellectual energy in the world today—even if that is rather a criticism of the present world. His gusto is gigantic, and in dialectical skill and virtuosity he has no rival. Not only are his novels philosophic, but he can make philosophy as exciting as any novel; he has brought philosophy from the schoolroom into the market-place (and even into more dubious areas) with a rush like a whirlwind—and good hard philosophy too! For Anglo-Saxons, however, this will not be enough to make him acceptable: they will want to know, Is he on the right side? Is he a force for Good? Phrases like " Beyond Good and Evil " or " If God is dead, all is permitted " fall flatly on English ears. A British writer who attacks current morality must make it clear, by his serious and anxious tone, that his intentions are pure. Otherwise, he may make smart people laugh—he may receive a fool's licence which deceives even himself—but he will be secretly disliked, and even despised. Only lately we have seen Bernard Shaw (compared with Sartre, a simple homespun moralist) fall completely from his hard-won popularity within a few months of his death. The English— like that other practical, unmetaphysical race, the Chinese— are fortunate, perhaps, in having a lay morality: a thing which scarcely exists on the continent of Europe, where morals are the province of the Churches (now wielding little

97

effective authority) or, latterly, of totalitarian States (which make a private conscience unnecessary and undesirable). In England the aristocracy—always a morally anarchic element—has been captured and tamed by the bourgeoisie, with the result that *la morale bourgeoise* appears under more attractive colours as " the conduct of a gentleman ". The disadvantage of killing the aristocrats is that their ghosts show an aptitude to walk, so that the bourgeois is seen always side by side with his wicked elder brother the courtier. The century of the naughty noblemen haunts the literary mind of France—even when the writer flirts, courtier-like, with the *canaille*; and there is no more written-about historic figure among French intellectuals today than the Marquis de Sade.

De Sade had virtues; outside of his particular neurosis, he appears to have been humane, and even quite remarkably magnanimous. During the Terror (when, as an old Bastille-prisoner, he was given high position) he used his influence on the side of mercy; and he spared the enemies who had ruined his whole life. Sartre, who to many of the French seems like a reincarnation of Sade, has very conspicuous virtues; compared with the Montherlants and the Drieu La Rochelles he is positively *sympathique*. He certainly hates tyranny and hypocrisy. Only, as we in this century have painfully learned, these much-advertised virtues can be ambiguous. One may dislike the sham because it is so unlike the real thing—or because it so much resembles it. One may hate the tyrant because he is tyrannical, or because after all he preserves some sort of order—because in fact he gets so little fun out of his possession of power.

On which side of the line are we to place Sartre? It is not easy to say; and he is enough of a Hegelian to revel in ambiguities. To be sure, no one can read (in *La Mort dans l'Ame*) his description of the common soldiers' agony when they learn that their officers have bolted by night, or the bitter remark of the Spanish general and ex-artist on being shown through a picture gallery in New York " One would need never to have fired upon men ", or his gentle character-isation of the resistants facing torture in *Morts sans Sépulture*, or the many fleeting snapshots he gives us of the " insulted and injured ", or the annihilating last close-up of *Le Sursis*— no one, I say, can read these passages without a quickening of the pulse, however tendentious they may be in their immediate purpose. Even the " heroes " in whom Sartre seems to put most of himself—Mathieu, Daniel Sereno, Roquentin—may be perverse, exasperating, degenerate, but they are not ignoble; their creator seems even to have the pleasant addiction of self-caricature. But there is some-thing about Sartre which makes us feel he would prefer the Nazi to the bourgeois liberal, the gangster to the *honnête homme*. There is a type of intellectual (common in France and not unknown elsewhere) who dislikes old tyrannies more than new ones because they are more naïve, even because they are more human. Such was, or almost was, Voltaire: he hated religion because it was cruel, but even more because he thought it silly. And Sartre is a modern Voltaire, with a disturbing streak of de Sade.

But there is also a third element in him, the most important —which brings him, in spite of all, into line with the certainly much greater Kierkegaard. He also is in his way a mystic, and has turned the minds of a whole generation of French-men to metaphysics. It is a conversion which the age of Anatole France could barely have imagined! Through Sartre, more than any man, the French have been inoculated with German philosophy, as—in an earlier era—were Turgeniev's Russians; but they have brought to it their clarity—and perhaps a slick efficiency—as the Russians brought an apocalyptic chaos. But in fact this development conforms well with the dramatic tendencies of the French mind. French thought seems to sway perpetually between libertarianism and a Jansenistic Catholicism; and the resulting tension gives to both their rather disconcerting harshness and acerbity. The real founder of the modern French propaganda-novel is the scatological mystic and unamiable humanitarian Léon Bloy, who was the spiritual begetter not only of Mauriac and Bernanos, but also a little of Céline— and Sartre. Of these writers only Sartre is a philosopher; but, whether they plump for the Pit or the Choir or (by turns) both, all of them are obsessed with *le Bien et le Mal* in a way that to an Englishman (for whom " the Good " is a practical matter merely, and a fairly simple one) seems just a little boring. Sartre's *Huis Clos* is perilously close to " Second Empire " in its Satanism; his *Le Diable et le Bon Dieu* almost smells of sulphur and red velvet.

It is an odd fact that while puritanism has died over much of Northern Europe (or changed into quite secular moralisms and depressions), the Jansenist heresy survives at the heart of French Catholicism, and even of French anti-clericalism, like a chilling drop of poison in a good glass of wine. In both it takes the form of an excessively sombre view of life, an insecurity in the realm of the non-logical, and a fascination with evil which seems often to fringe on melodrama. Baudelaire and Gautier, Flaubert and Maupassant—these were not Catholics nor in any true sense Pagans; they were (unsuspected by themselves) spiritually Jansenists. Only, living in a prosaic materialistic environment with a nostalgia of the old régime, these imaginative artists created a new Devil—the Bourgeois. And, as the republican bourgeoisie were in certain respects oddly puritan—or at least prudish— their Jansenistic denouncers appeared (naturally, much to their own delight) like wicked diabolists, as their successors today are still well content to appear. That is the paradox, and in a social sense the malady, of France. And I think it is the paradox, and the dangerousness, of Jean-Paul Sartre.

Sartre scarifies the bourgeois as Shaw scarified the

" Victorians " (which is perhaps the nearest English ana-
logue of this unpopular concept). Shaw, however, wanted
to *reform* the Victorians, and to a large extent he succeeded,
if not always quite in the ways he wished; but Sartre, a
rebel in the Continental root-and-branch tradition, does not
at all care about reforming anyone. He has not the least
idea of what sort of society he wants; he is not really a communist but (what is something both better and worse) an
anarchist—and he can have few illusions as to what would
be his fate in a leftist *coup d'état*. Moreover the bourgeoisie
is necessary to him, as the Jews were to Hitler; if the bourgeois did not exist, Sartre would have to invent him. The
French, by their very suppleness of mind, are more wedded
to the *word* than any other people; and it is the word which
ties *concepts* to *things* (including those weary concepts, the
absolute Good and Evil) like a restrictive gold standard.
Thus we have the strange contradiction that a very intelligent
nation will always be, mentally, rather static and in arrear
of the *Zeitgeist*; we have seen how France is consciously very
eighteenth century, and subconsciously even seventeenth
century. Sartre's Existentialism appears as a revolt against
the philosophy of the absolute—he denounces it as " bad
faith " and " the spirit of seriousness ", its upholders are
salauds; but struggle as he may in his squirrel-cage, he
can only make the bars revolve more dizzily. Beneath all
the queer Teutonic vocables, he has set up a new Good and
Evil of *Freedom* and *Nature*—concepts which, thus opposed,
mean only a vague restlessness and a vague disgust.

In an impressive, often-quoted, passage in *What is
Literature?* Sartre wrote,

It is neither our fault nor our merit if we lived at a time
when torture was a daily fact. Chateaubriand, Oradour,
the Rue des Saussaies, Dachau and Ausschwitz have all
demonstrated to us that evil is not an appearance. . . . Five
years. We lived in a daze, and as we did not take our

profession of writer lightly, this state of shock is still reflected in our writings. We have undertaken to create a literature of extreme situations. . . . We are Jansenists because the age has made us such.

And elsewhere in the same work he says: " All war is a form of Manicheism ". This is no doubt true—though the language is that of " plain man's " pathos rather than Existentialist logic, and none the worse for that. The moral, one would think, is that the philosopher should hate war, especially civil war, and the black-out of the mind which war brings. Still, let us grant the Sartrian doctrine (a sound one on the whole, and in the case referred to undoubtedly a very courageous one) that the writer should take up a position[1]; we have seen that the recognition of vital tensions is what is valuable in Existentialism. Sartre's Jansenism or Manicheism, or however the personification of Evil be called, is deeper (and showed itself earlier) than the French Underground movement; it produced comedy in *La Nausée* as it produced melodrama (though fine melodrama) in

---

[1] It is obvious that the doctrine of " engagement " is as dangerous as the " indifference " of the Yogi; in practice it can mean the communist heresy that art should be propaganda. Mr. MacNeice has written (in *The Poetry of W. B. Yeats*): " The propagandist is only interested in changing the world; any use of words therefore which will lead to that end—lies, distortions or outrageous simplifications—will, from his point of view, be true. This is a tenable position but . . ." It is not at all a tenable position, except for a demented fanatic. Nevertheless I find these words of Sartre admirable: " I hold Flaubert and Gautier responsible for the repression which followed the Commune, because they did not write a line to prevent it. It will be said, it was not their business. But was the trial of Calas Voltaire's business? Was the condemnation of Dreyfus Zola's business? Was the administration of the Congo Gide's business? Each of these authors, at a particular moment of his life, measured his responsibility as a writer. The Occupation has taught us ours. *Since we act upon our time by our very existence, we decide that our action shall be deliberate* ".—*Les Temps Modernes*, October 1945. (Italics mine.) The last sentence is truly great—like the saying of Jaspers after the Nazi beastliness, " *Dass wir noch leben ist unsere Schuld.*" (It is our guilt that we still live.)

Morts sans Sépulture. Sartre, though his perceptions are vivid and even (in a cathartic, surrealist sense) poetic, is a Manichee in the strict sense of a matter-hater[1]; Nature, for him, is the ugly, and beauty is purely subjective. He is the opposite of a Chesterton or a Lawrence to whom the very independence and strangeness of Nature appear rich and thrilling—who delight in the *density* of matter as though in the consistency of a fruit, or who feel the earth as the Great Goddess. Sartre could not write like Lawrence:

Cézanne's apple is a great deal more than Plato's Idea. Cézanne's apple rolled the stone from the mouth of the tomb. . . . The man of flesh has been slowly destroyed through centuries to give place to the man of spirit, the mental man, the self-conscious I. And in his soul Cézanne knew it, and wanted to rise in the flesh.[2]

For Sartre, the flesh is merely *le visqueux*, a kind of monstrous growth. He does not hate sadistic torturers so much as he hates the body, which can suffer torture—even the torture of being " transfixed ", like an insect under a pin, by a chance *Look*.

For if the key-word in Kierkegaard is *despair*, and in Heidegger *dread*, that of Sartre is not really the one or the other, but *disgust*—though a disgust which implies a certain metaphysical humility, as of a small man in a crowd. (The fact that Sartre is personally surprisingly small must not be overlooked!) In *La Nausée*, the hero Roquentin—himself a very deracinated intellectual—sits under a chestnut-tree in a park, contemplating one of the tree's dark thick

---

[1] " A discreet and insurmountable nausea perpetually reveals the body to consciousness. . . . Far from our having to understand this term *nausea* as a metaphor derived from our physiological disgusts, it is on the contrary against this background that are produced all the concrete and empirical nauseas (nauseas at the sight of rotten meat, fresh blood, excrements, etc.) which lead us to being sick."—*L'Etre et le Néant*. One notes the queer use of *Gestalt* terminology.

[2] *Introduction to His Paintings.*

roots; one thinks of the sage Gautama under the bo-tree, or Omar and his book of verses beneath the bough. Suddenly he has an " illumination ", which " takes his breath away ". The innocent reader expects (and is doubtless intended to expect) some mystical rapture; but the emotion that has flooded over Roquentin is in fact nauseated disgust. The tree *exists*—gratuitously, without any reason, exists! No logical necessity can explain or justify it. The mere " facticity ", the " contingency ", of the tree is unbearable. This of course makes amusing reading, but the truth is that Roquentin (or rather Sartre—for we are not told that Roquentin was an *agrégé*) has his head full of Hegel, and the whole passage might have been written as a skit upon the Master, whose diatribes against Nature it resembles. If one were to treat it seriously, one might point out that Roquentin, in a French municipal park, was scarcely considering Nature under one of her more advantageous or significant aspects. But taken by itself, who would think that this professorial fooling was to be made the basis of that formidable 700-page " Essay in Phenomenological Ontology ", *Being and Nothing*?

Nature now becomes the *être-en-soi* (*An-sich-sein*), Heidegger's *Seiendes*—Hegelianised as the object (though an unattainable one) of man's striving; though it also has affinities with the One Substance of Spinoza, and even the Value-concept (" a homogeneous jelly ") of Marx. (Sartre's world, as contrasted with Heidegger's, has a Classical substantiality, and resembles rather a rotted fruit.) Heidegger's *Dasein* has become the *être-pour-soi* (*Für-sich-sein*), but lacking almost all transcendental unity: it is in fact the *En-Soi* which approximates to the Teutonic " Absolute ". The *Pour-Soi* has *Existence*, but not *Essence* or true *Being*—its existence is a paradox Being, negative in relation to itself (because it always *wants*, and in that sense *is*, what it is not), negative in relation to the *En-Soi* (because it must distinguish itself from the world in the acts of willing and knowing), negative in relation to its own *Néant* or state of " splitness " (because it must continually transcend the *here* in knowing and the *now* in willing)[1]. To all this I find little to object; it is a restatement, in phenomenological terms, of what all religions have affirmed in their fashion—the special or somehow exceptional nature of Man: even if Sartre expresses it, paradoxically, by denying to Man a " nature ". If Sartre had said nothing else than this he would be an interesting thinker; but of course he has said many other things—good, not-so-good and plain bad—even within the covers of *L'Etre et le Néant*. Sartre accurately shows how the human being is lured by an impossible aim: to cease from striving without relinquishing consciousness—to capture for itself an Essence and Being—in short to become the God of which it has dreamed, perhaps still dreams.[2] Such a hope is the very meaning of the Future—which, as we know, " never comes ", but exists, like Death in Heidegger's phrase (but more truly) as an " impossible possibility ". That, to put it shortly, is man's ironical freedom—the freedom forever to seek an unattainable freedom. Again, a truth that needs

[1] Sartre draws up a list of " negativities " which include absence, alteration, otherness, repulsion, regret, distraction, etc. All these perceptions inspire a feeling akin to dread. My friend's absence from the café haunts it like a ghost. This distinguishes positive negation (so to call it) from mere logical negation. All of which seems to me to be true; and the difficulty of stating it without (apparent) absurdity, a measure of the failure of mere " abstract " thought. When French Existentialists speak of the " Absurd ", they mean the insufficiency of the logical explanation. Nations which have believed less in logic are less likely to be perturbed.

[2] In different words, everyone sets before himself an ideal, X, which he or she aspires to be. But to be X and at the same time oneself is a logical impossibility; and if X is associated with a real person, that person aspires similarly to be Y. The idealisations X and Y are merely (as Sartre would express it) " magical concepts," self-contradictory in themselves. And yet such idealisation—Sartre rightly emphasises—is part of the very structure of human consciousness.

saying and again saying, if we are to guard ourselves from
" enthusiasms " (such as the utopian socialism which Sartre
himself seems to have espoused). But Sartre, who cuts all
the strings binding his Hegelian concepts, has foundered
in a pessimism which is too absolute. The Synthesis is not
in an unqualified sense attainable, the dialectic is not
irreversible; in short perfectibility is an empty dream—
progress even may be an illusion. But human existence *may*,
approximately, capture an " essence "; it is what is called in
a person *character*[1] and in a people *culture* (and Sartre, if he
knew it, would value higher the achievements of culture).
The fission in self-consciousness and the tension in self-will,
though always no doubt present, are felt chiefly at adoles-
cence and in epochs of transition. Roquentin looking at the
chestnut-tree had an essence (even if only " sketched in ")
as the chestnut-tree had an essence; it was his essence to
loathe chestnut-trees, as it is part of the essence of other men
to like them—or, more often, to think they like them, and
never really to see them. For Roquentin at least *looked at* the
chestnut-tree; he had the " root " of the happy contempla-
tive nature in him. And we shall see that the Look, with its
startling possibilities, is Sartre's really vital contribution to
philosophy.

But one may suspect that Sartre's pessimism is a deduction
from his " Manicheism "—a deduction which seems fully
justified. If Nature is always as repulsive as he holds (and he
seems to regard his repulsion as the normal reaction) why
indeed should the human existence battle to possess itself of a

---

[1] It is true that this is to some extent a matter of terms, as Sartre
recognises a " fundamental project " or " organic totality of projects "
(while he identifies the *character* with the body or mere " facticity ").
Sartre would say that Kierkegaard left Regine, not because that was his
" character ", but because he wanted to write the sort of books arising
out of such a situation. This may well have been his unconscious motive,
only I submit that we do not know. In other words, a character—like a
tree—has always an element of mystery.

" nature "? How would the *Pour-Soi* be advanced by uniting itself with an *En-Soi*?[1] To what end this *mariage de convenance*? Hegel had excellently shown that Being and Nothing, if not merged in their synthesis Becoming, tend to step into each other's shoes; and in Sartre—for whom this synthesis is no more than an illusion, though an ontologically necessary one—there seems little to choose between them. Both *En-Soi* and *Pour-Soi* are absurd,[2] gratuitous, *de trop*—the whole arsenal of Existentialist Billingsgate is employed against them both. *Angoisse*, for Sartre, is barely distinguishable from *Nausée*; the former term indeed (borrowed from Heidegger) he seldom uses without an apology for its " solemnity "—almost a wink at the reader. And rightly, for nowhere do his heroes show a trace of the tragic responsibility which Sartre, in one of his works, preaches. Mathieu's conception of freedom is like Roquentin's feeling about the chestnut-sucker: almost that of a cancer, gnawing the entrails of Being, or " a worm in the core of a fruit ". (The unpleasant image of " gnawing " is also Bergson's.) It is simply an irrational *datum*, infuriating to a mild teacher of philosophy; and, to be rid of it, Mathieu gets himself killed in a quite pointless skirmish—only ennobled by the democratic camaraderie which is Sartre's finest quality. Sartre the moralist convicts the *salauds* of *mauvaise foi*, but Sartre the philosopher (by a slight shift of meanings, which is itself a piece of bad faith ordinarily so called) shows *mauvaise foi* to be inseparable from the human condition. (This is because the *Pour-soi*, i.e. man, can never be at unity with himself; but it seems perverse to

---

[1] One might even say, if the idea of God is contemptible (as Sartre by his virulent atheism suggests), why should man wish to become God? Why can he not take the Eastern road of life-denial, recommended by Schopenhauer? If on the other hand the nostalgia for Deity, though hopeless, is not contemptible, why should the theists be deserving of contempt for giving this symbolisation to the Perfect?

[2] It comes almost as a shock to remember that Kierkegaard, by " the Absurd ", had meant the Incarnation.

describe such lack of internal harmony as " bad faith ".)
Such statements as " the Nothing is nihilated " have, we
have seen, a true meaning when they are understood—even
if the logical positivist, with a dreadfully superior air, would
shrug them away as " pseudo-statements ". But Sartre, one
cannot but feel, derives great satisfaction from their nihilistic
flavour. He points them at us like the nasty juvenile of his
story *Erostrate*, pointing his automatic at the prostitute.

However that may be, the happy condition of a *Pour-Soi-
En-Soi* (Hegel's rather alarming *An-und-für-sichselbstigkeit*) is
an idle hope—though a hope without which Time would
stop. Man, for Sartre, is a " useless passion ", who " destroys
himself in vain that God may be born ". On the other
hand, the *Pour-Soi* is in ceaseless peril of returning to the
state of a contingent *En-Soi* (meaning, a mere *thing*); a fate
which he can scarcely avoid while he lives among men, and
which is bound to overtake him, in any case, at his death.
This happens through the agency of that formidable factor
in life *Autrui*, who now enters the picture; and it is here that
L'Etre et le Néant casts away in fact from the " phenomenological ontology " of the sub-title for the broad seas of
intuition. Sartre advances what he considers to be a disproof
of solipsism—that shadow, like the chasm of Pascal, which
has menaced philosophy for three centuries. To be conscious
of *being perceived*, Sartre argues (to put it in a sentence), is as
primary and fundamental as to *perceive*. Logically this
scarcely seems sufficient, for one may *dream* (with terror) that
one is being perceived; and for the solipsist, life is a larger
dream. But upon the turbid subject of dreams I have no
wish or competence to embark. On the other hand there are
persons, Sartre himself tells us, so hardened in indifference
as to live their lives without experiencing the Other—" ex-
cepting only in rare, terrifying, illuminations." Practical
solipsists, they treat their fellows as " walls ", " obstacles ",
or mere " coefficients of adversity ". Yet, one must grant,

the fact that a person is *two* people—a subject and an object —surely proves that he can never be *alone*, or a *Pour-Soi-En-Soi*; after that, the existence of *others* is mere extension. Sartre is therefore saying something important[1]; though it is marred, as usual, by much that is dubious or repulsive. Indeed, *L'Etre et le Néant* might almost better have been titled *Moi et l'Autre*. Descartes had said, " I think, therefore I am ", but he did not say " I feel, therefore I am "—which he should have done, for feeling is prior to thought; and his emphasis on the *knowable* was a misfortune. Sartre, who beneath all his Teutonisms remains basically a Cartesian, takes the formula a step farther; he says in effect "I can feel *malaise*, therefore there is someone who is Not-I that causes it "—though this inference is the logic of feeling and not of thinking. The Self now becomes aware of its own limits through its awareness of the Not-Self, the Other—it is almost " I feel, therefore *Another* is ", and finally (as Daniel says in *Le Sursis*): " I am seen, therefore I am ". What the Mirror, we have fancied, was for the young Kierkegaard, the Observer's Medusa-Eye is for Sartre[2]: it represents the

[1] How would a serious solipsist (if such a person could be found) reply to Sartre's " disproof "? Somewhat, I imagine, like this: " I am not so foolish as to maintain that other consciousnesses like mine are inconceivable. I merely see no reason to believe that they, in fact, exist, and are not mere projections of my self-consciousness; and it will need better arguments than Sartre's to make me change my opinion. That is, supposing—for the sake of this pleasant little argument I am having with myself—that you, Sir, and your friend M. Sartre are real people ". One can fancy Kierkegaard's father talking so, in one of those imaginary dialogues; and one realises (almost with a shock) that Sartre also draws some of his life from that patriarch's dreams.

[2] Sartre continually thinks of the Eye of God in this manner, which may help to explain the extraordinary bitterness of his atheism: in spite of the fact that humanity (he holds) must fail to become *one*, lacking an Ultimate Observer, and that he regards this failure as part of the human tragedy. To quote from his Daniel of *Les Chemins de la Liberté:* " The Medusa-Look will fall from on high, petrifying. . . . Virtues of stone, vices of stone: what comfort! Those people have well-proven techniques. . . . You look at me and all hope dies: I am tired of fleeing. But I know

Uncanny, the Equivocal—the shock which splinters our homely universe into a "multiverse", wherein we are *afraid*. In Sartre's words, "With the Other's look the situation escapes me, or, to use a familiar expression, I am no longer master of the situation ".

Sartre, however, just for fear we should take him seriously, at once proceeds to cheapen and sensationalise his idea. Suppose, he says, I am doing something held to be discreditable—say listening at a key-hole. Suddenly I become aware of an *eye* behind me, fixing me—perhaps an accusing voice and outstretched finger. For the first time I experience, along with terror, *shame;* and Sartre will have it that all guilt-feelings originated in this way—a very obvious cart-before-horse argument. In his massive analysis of Genet, the pederast and thief of genius (where the vision of the accusing finger is again called up), we find something like the ancient theory that it is the Law which brings Sin into the world, and not the other way; and it is suggested that the thief (who was not one until he was detected) does well to take up the challenge, and show that one Absolute of conduct is as good—or bad—as another.[1] The thesis is

that beneath your Eye I can no longer flee ". Or again: " To tell you what the *Look* is would be easy for me, for it is nothing; it is an absence. Imagine the darkest night. It is the night that looks at you—but a dazzling night, the night in broad light, the secret night of the day. I stream with black light, I have it everywhere on my hands, on my eyes, on my heart, and I do not see it. You may believe that this perpetual violation at first was odious to me ". One recalls very similar passages in the works of D. H. Lawrence.

[1] Sartre seems to use the rhetorical phrase *for eternity* in a double sense —implying, on the one hand, that thief or pederast must continue in their vicious courses once they have been seen and judged, and that their judges should blame themselves: and, on the other, that their " essences "—created by the Look—must remain forever fixed in the Time-process, like statues in a corridor, even after the man has gone on to found new " essences ". This confusion is another instance of the " bad faith " which we find so often in Sartre—the attempt to turn sound metaphysical points into rather unsound moral or sociological ones.

advanced with Shavian brilliance, but with a " tough " cynicism that Shaw would have found incredible, and a perversity of imagination unprecedented, I should think, in the literature of ideas. (Nevertheless, though the book is scarcely likely to be translated, it has pages which show Sartre's bitter raillery at its best.)

The Fall, for Heidegger (as we saw), meant man's falling into the world. For Sartre it means his falling among other men: almost literally indeed " among thieves ", for every eye is like a looking-glass in a death-chamber, liable (as primitive men hold) to steal the soul in transit. Thus the world becomes a gallery of mirrors, turned at all imaginable angles to catch the victim. The Eye for Sartre is almost the opposite of what it was for Berkeley—it gives death and not life. The Other transfixes me, petrifies me, " em-pastes " me, " en-glues " me: he " steals my world ", draws it out of shape like a new magnet appearing in my magnetic field. The Other's Look causes in me a " hæmorrhage " whereby my world leaks away, so that in an average twenty-four hours I must suffer as many wounds as St. Sebastian. The harmless citizen on his social round is disintegrated daily into a hundred fragments: or, in Sartrian terms, his existence is solidified into a hundred " essences ". The Self is a characterless " sitter "; but every day he most pose for a hundred cameramen, and assume varying features on the photographic plate of the retina. He is a mere liquidity, poured by turn into a hundred diversely shaped containers. In short, he is always alone, and yet always an " Other ". Sartre has progressed but one step beyond monism—and fallen into an idealistic pluralism.

This is the meaning of the famous L'enfer, c'est les autres, and it certainly seems as if, for Sartre, happiness is only to be sought in blind asylums. Yet it would have been easy to give his idea an attractive, or at least not exclusively distressing, form[1]. The good actor may be a motley to the view of the groundlings, but he is something more to the better critics. The normal person, after all, is not always doing things of which he need be ashamed—a spyer at key-holes, himself observed by other spies as it were through other key-holes, and so on endlessly like the figures in a Ripolin advertisement. A man caught in an unfortunate moment, it is true, will feel all that Sartre has so well described. The moment before he seemed to himself the master of the universe, the next moment he is as if turned to water and sucked (if you care to put it so) down the drainpipe of another consciousness. In short he is, as we say, *embarrassed*, but it seems unnatural to describe the situation of man among other men as a perpetual embarrassment. Sartre has in fact combined the Husserlite doctrine of " outward reference " with his Manichean hatred of the body; one wonders if he had laid upon him, in childhood, the old injunction to be " seen and not heard " (under which he can have been no patient subject). Yet for beings not deformed or ill-conditioned, the Other's Look is not seldom pleasant and encouraging—however much such encouragement may partake of deception or " *mauvaise foi* ". The (literally) eternal triangle in *Huis Clos* was, of course, bound to be a horror; for three is, generally speaking, an impossible

[1] Sartre's determination to draw the unnatural conclusion is shown again in the passage about the waiter (*L'Etre et le Néant*, p. 98). The waiter (whom he amusingly describes) only *plays* at being a waiter, because the *Pour-Soi* " is what it is not and is not what it is "—and this is given as an instance of that *mauvaise foi* which is the special guilt or tragedy of man. (Similarly with all other human professions and types: the soldier plays at being a soldier, and even the coward only plays at running away.) The weakness of this argument, on M. Sartre's own premisses, is that it is wholly Platonist or " essentialist ". There is no Ideal Waiter or Ideal Coward whom the real human being is copying: if there were such a thing as a robot waiter, it would rather be the automaton that was copying the man. However, the fact that there is an element of " acting " in all human acts is no doubt true and well observed; and I altogether refuse to be depressed by it.

number. Hell is not the Other, but (as every " only child " knows) the Third; and, with symbolic rightness, only one member of the trio in *Huis Clos* is evil. (In spite of his adolescent interest in perversity, Sartre seldom presents us with really evil types.) Wherever three persons are gathered together, there will be found to be perpetual groupings and regroupings of the evens against the odds, or the frustrated sense of " How happy could I be with either ". But two, how- ever ill-assorted, can make shift with one another: the game of " transcending " their mutual " transcendences " (in short, learning to know each other) can be pleasurable— even if its complete success would spoil the pleasure. Sartre would perhaps reply that there is always the third; and this seeming flippancy *à la française* no doubt contains a truth. It is the Third—the Hegelian Antithesis—who is the agent of fermentation and change. But there is almost no mention of him (or indeed of the Dialectic) in *L'Etre et le Néant*. In that book we are told only of *Moi* and *l'Autre*: two persons of unspecified sex and as abstract as X and Y, who—without even the factor of jealousy—are doomed, in love, to a perpetual checkmate.

It is typical of the violence of Existentialist phraseology that the word " appropriation " is used for every movement of thought or action (and for Existentialism, as for Pragmat- ism, the two are one). Just as faith, for Kierkegaard, was " a passionate appropriation of the objectively uncertain ", so the Sartrian *Pour-Soi* appropriates (i.e. fashions and moulds) its world. Heidegger had used the term " dis-covery ", but his meaning was the same; indeed Sartre—who allows Nature qualities, though not meanings—is the more " realist " of the two[1]. For these philosophers Truth is an intact virgin,

---

[1] This follows from the fact that the *Pour-Soi* is a mere " lack ". (Although, in Heidegger, the active subject appeared sometimes as *das Nichts*, it received—as with most of the Germans—the whole of the em- phasis.) The most that the Sartrian *Pour-Soi* can do is to cut up the world into patterns and string it out along perspectives, by means of its

ceasing to be true in the moment of being possessed—or, what is the same thing, becoming true for the first time in that moment. Sartre's words deserve to be quoted:

> To the degree to which I appear to myself as *creating* objects by the sole relation of appropriation, these objects are *myself*. The fountain-pen and the pipe, the dress, the desk, the house—they are I. The totality of my possessions reflects the totality of my being. I *am* that which I *have*. *It is I* whom I touch on this cup, on this trinket. This mountain which I climb is *myself* to the degree to which I overcome it; and when I am at its summit, which I have " acquired " at the cost of these same efforts, this wide view over the valley and the surrounding peaks is again *myself*. The panorama is myself expanded to the horizon, for it exists only through me, for me.[1]

Even the poor scientist, hunched over his microscope, is, for Sartre, a deflowerer and a devourer; Sartre has invented for him an " Actæon-complex " (Actæon stealing through the bushes to surprise a bathing nymph) and even a " Jonah-complex "—though it should surely be a Whale-complex! " If one examines the comparisons commonly used to express the relationship of the knower and the known, one sees that many of them present themselves as a certain *violation by the view*. The unknown object is given as immaculate, as virgin . . . One tears the veils from Nature." " The works of French epistemology swarm with alimentary ever-shifting "projects". One observes constantly in Sartre the influence of the Gestalt psychologists. At the same time Sartre seems greatly to overstress projects, and to undervalue qualities, in the constitution of the world; one scarcely supposes that Picasso sees objects quite as he paints them, even while he is projecting a picture! The eighteenth-century divine bred on Paley, who thought that rabbits had been given white bobtails to convenience short-sighted sportsmen, would have been (merely with the substitution of the human subject for God) a good Sartrian.

[1] *L'Etre et le Néant*, pp. 680-1. Sartre sees this self-imprisonment as the tragedy of the Divine Creator (if He existed)—a conception which is one of Sartre's probably unconscious debts to Gnosticism.

metaphors—absorption, digestion, assimilation." Even more alarming, " destruction " we are told " realises appropriation perhaps more subtly than creation, for the object destroyed is no longer there to show itself impenetrable. . . . The flames that consume the farm to which I have set fire realise little by little the fusion of the farm with myself: by being annihilated it converts itself into *me*.[1] " It would seem to be the problem-child of *Erostrate* who is writing. Such passages, which may be remembered among the curiosities of human thought, are no doubt meant to shock—but they shock us only into laughter.

Naturally the attitudes of sexual love—in the ordinary sense—are, for Sartre, no exception to the rule; with this difference, that in love I seek to appropriate not an object (or not an object only) but a subject—not a *thing* but a *freedom*. Sexuality is the supreme attempt (fated, like every other attempt, to frustration) to " found my facticity "— or, in ordinary language, to acquire a reason and justification for my existence. Kierkegaard could find that foundation in God's love, though nowhere else; even for Heidegger there is a shadow of the transcendental in the *Mitsein*. But for Sartre there can be, of course, nothing of the kind; " The essence of the relations between consciousnesses is not the *Mitsein*, it is conflict ". We must remember, however, that for Sartre such conflict is of a peculiar kind: it is above all a flight from the Other's ominous *Eye*— his truly " evil eye "— a flight which is driven to take the form of pursuit. The best form of defence, in a word, is attack: *le Pour-Soi* (as Sartre puts it, in one of his neat jingling phrases) *est poursuivant-poursuivi*. Just as (we have seen) I " create ", and in fact *am*, my fountain-pen or my pipe, so the Other—who

---

[1] *L'Etre et le Néant*, p. 683. Even generosity, it appears, is a form of the lust for possession. " This rage of destruction which underlies generosity is nothing else but a rage to possess." Should one be glad—or not—that M. Sartre is, as one knows, a generous man?

sees me—creates me, endows me with an outside and an *essence*. By capturing the Other (" transcending " his " transcendence ") I capture my own dimension of Otherness. This I can only do, or attempt to do, through a sort of duel of *être-regardant* and *être-regardé*.[1] And, unfortunately, the attempt must fail.

Sartre divides sex-relations into four basic patterns, which lead from one to another by logical necessity—love, masochism, desire, sadism; and also (following on the failure of these conducts) a fifth, namely hate. All other human relationships—maternal love, pity, loyalty to a cause or a sovereign—are, for him, mere variations on these themes. The English reader will mutter " Freud ", but Sartre, the Husserlite, will not hear of an Unconscious. Some people are in *mauvaise foi*, that is all. Sartre's constant tone of a scolding schoolmaster, somewhat recalling Bernard Shaw, is largely due to this denial. Love, for Sartre, consists in the single aim of capturing the Other's love; it must fail because the Other, naturally, will be animated by a similar sole ambition—so that love becomes a circle of X wanting Y to want X to want Y. Masochism is the attempt to capture the Other, failing his love, through his thirst for power—by making of myself a passive object; but my attempt—being based on deliberate calculation—must fail, like the effort to put oneself to sleep by force of will. The client in a brothel who pays a woman to beat him is clearly the user, not the used. One remembers the difficulties encountered by the ingenious Sacher-Masoch, in prevailing on ladies to maltreat him. " Desire," which curiously comes third on the list, seeks to compass the same object by *merging;* unable to overcome the opposite number, I try to drag him or her with me into fleshliness—in Sartre's language, " to reduce the Other to his simple facticity, but to make of his facticity a perpetual

[1] It is surprising that Sartre nowhere, to my knowledge, discusses hypnotic phenomena.

presentation of its nihilating transcendence ". My caressing hand, in imitation of my eye, will seek to sculpt the Other's flesh; I seek to " en-glue " his liberty in his flesh, to capture it like a wolf in the sheep-pen, like the armed men in the Trojan horse. Again, a self-contradictory aim—unrealisable, among other reasons, because desire has its natural consummation. There remains sadism. The object of sadism is " the immediate appropriation of the facticity of the other ". The sadist seeks for the moment when his victim " is entirely flesh, panting and obscene; it keeps the position that the torturers have given to it " (note the sudden transference to the plural) " not that which it would have taken by itself; the cords which bind it sustain it as an inert thing and, by that very fact, it has ceased to be an object which moves spontaneously ". But alas, the persevering *Pour-Soi* is foiled again. The victim can *look* at his tormentor, or tormentors, and their whole enterprise collapses.[1] (Since we are in the world of shockerdom, one may ask why Sartre ignores an obvious possibility—namely that the rather improbably susceptible torturers may have taken the precaution of blinding their victims.[2])

[1] English readers will be reminded of *The Ancient Mariner*:
> " An orphan's curse would drag to Hell
> A spirit from on high;
> But oh! more horrible than that
> Is a curse in a dead man's eye! "

[2] Much may be forgiven to Sartre having regard to his experience of the Occupation, when (as he says) " torture was a daily fact ", and during which he bravely associated himself with the Resistance. At the same time it must be remembered that *L'Etre et le Néant* was written (a surprising feat) during the few months of his captivity after the *débâcle*—that is to say, before the severities of the Gestapo had commenced, so far as France was concerned. One does not want to throw doubts on M. Sartre's humanity, but the fact that he can be sympathetic to Russian totalitarianism (with its liquidations, prison camps, and all the usual features of dictatorship) is, as M. Camus has pointed out, somewhat disturbing. Sartre is so ignorant of the European reality that he can say the deportations after the war in Eastern Europe were a

But we are not yet at the end. The *Pour-Soi* has another trick up its sleeve. A failure in love, desire, masochism and sadism, it will try *hate*; and for a Sartre it would seem, as for Shylock,[1] hate will not stop short of murder. Despairing of capturing the Other's freedom, I will endeavour to " suppress " him. But this is the most futile procedure of all, for in extirpating him (apart from the fact that I still *need* him for my projects) I send him into the grave with all his wrong views of me uncorrected, and eternally unmodifiable—a casket to which I have thrown away the key.[2] Thus I am forever " contaminated " by the Other in my very being— " even if the Other should have been entirely overcome " Never will the Other now be able to write that letter of apology, to stretch out his hand to me, to confess frankly " You were right and I was wrong "; never will I be able to speak the (once possibly) healing words! A mournful thought which must have occurred to many of us, on various occasions, at the funerals of our friends—whether or not we happened to have murdered them.

This happy sketch of human relations, which would have surprised most people at almost any time before the 1930s, is not altogether without interest[3]; and Sartre does well to remind us that " sadism " and " masochism "—the instinct of power and the instinct of self-abasement—are elements

lesser evil than the colour bar in America! M. Sartre's sympathy with the negro is praiseworthy, but is it fanciful to connect it with a realisation that he is himself an *âme noire?* French romanticism can play some curious tricks.

[1] " Hates any man the thing he would not kill? " Or, for that matter, woman. Françoise, the sympathetic heroine of Simone de Beauvoir's novel *L'Invitée*, is of this mind.

[2] Ægistheus in *Les Mouches* expresses the same thought: "The dead have ceased to be, and that is why they have made themselves the incorruptible guardians of your crimes ".

[3] In particular, one notes this excellent observation: " Vice is, essentially, the love of frustration ". But, in Sartre's system, might not this be a definition of life?

in all sexual love, even when they are unconscious ones. Love is never, in fact, merely physical. That is the reason why the Don Juan, so often sentimentalised as a seeker of the Ideal, and his co-relative, the *allumeuse*, are slightly devilish; they are enslavers, and call out the base instinct of self-enslavement. And that again is why philosophies like Jansenism and Manicheism, which derive a morose delectation from making the body an object—whether to stimulate or to suppress it—are a little equivocal also. But it is surely confusing to use the language of clinical literature for impulses that are universal and, within certain limits, quite normal and unavoidable: as if one should call the inveterate book-borrower a " kleptomaniac ". Sadists and masochists, in the technical sense, are happily rare; and in fact the examples given by Sartre seem drawn from prison camps, and a certain class of brothels, rather than from the practice of the generality of lovers. For the same reason, they are not philosophically interesting. And I cannot but think the prodigious sales of *L'Etre et le Néant* (a book for the most part incomprehensible to all but a very few) must be due to this Sartrian ingredient of sensationalism.

. . . . .

Sartre is the greatest philosopher of the *Outside*—of that dimension of the Self which is forever hidden from us, which even the actor can only guess at when he reads his Press notices in the cold morning. And Sartre can make us feel, very vividly, that we are all actors—in a play which we improvise as we go along, and in which nobody is a privileged spectator. If the play seems to us a poor one, we cannot blame author, producer or critic; for each of us is all three. No one like Sartre makes us realise the shock of the perceiver being perceived—the miracle that occurs as often as our cosy " visual field " is invaded by an alien consciousness. In his godless world, which is after all our modern world, the understanding eye of Omniscience is replaced by a myriad merciless or careless eyes. This is an experience, indeed a truth, which it is necessary to face and imaginatively to comprehend. It is no good dismissing it as exaggerated self-consciousness, for such self-consciousness is a condition of man's present " mental age ".[1] Every man is two men—I do not mean a soul and a body, for the traditional " soul " was conceived as just another *thing*—but a subject and an object. Subject X can only know Object Y, Subject Y can only know Object X—and themselves, the two *Néants*, they can never know. They can only know and possess, so to speak, a shadow of each other—the Other's *outside*. Each man is divided from his " I " by the screen of *the other person*—as a project in time and an object in space: " It is he [the Other] who intervenes between me and myself " (*The Journey and the Return*). Of that thin film-world, that wide but insubstantial territory, I am the sole possessor; here my eye can lord it, and what more natural than that the Other should resent my freedom, and use every means to frustrate it—ranging from the arts of love to sadism and murder? It is only the lowest man—the mass-man—who, by his assimilation to the *En-Soi*, can know himself approximately as he is.

Sartre, I say, is the philosopher of frustration—the discoverer, almost, of our eternal limit and obstruction, the *Outside*. We should not complain if he is, judged by the highest standards, superficial, for he is haunted and tortured by the impenetrability of surfaces. *The Other* is for him that which Death is for Heidegger, what the " Paradox " of Faith was for Kierkegaard—the necessary cross which we

[1] Hence, perhaps, the common plaintive modern desire to be " understood ". The converted Daniel in *Le Sursis* expresses himself thus: " What joy, what torture, I am at last changed into myself! I am hated, despised, tolerated—but a presence sustains me in being forever. I am infinite and infinitely guilty—but I *am*, I am. Before God and before men, I *am*! "

carry, the price of our incarnation. Why then does Sartre's analysis of human relationships, similarly to Heidegger's analysis of human effort, seem to miss something? Why, in fact, does it affect us as almost comically insufficient? The fallacy of Heidegger, we saw, was to confound the individual with the Absolute; but Sartre is too much of a French novelist (and a Cartesian) to have much time for the Absolute. Sartre's fault is very nearly the opposite; for him the individual, defined as a *Néant*, exists in a strange void. Sartre's protagonists seem always to be shooting at one another from behind cover; they never come out into the open or see each other's faces.[1] One would scarcely guess, from any of his writings, that human beings are fathers, mothers, children (in fact the personages of his fiction are usually Malthusians!). Similarly we notice, in his account of sex relations, that he has not dealt at all with *real* people, or even with males and females, but with two *Pour-Sois*—two identical skeletons; no reason is ever hinted at why, among all the people in the world, *this* person should be concerned with *that* person.[2] But if Sartre had asked himself this question he would have discovered an odd fact: namely that though Subject X cannot (directly) know himself, he can discover much about Subject Y, and incidentally about himself, through the study of Object Y—a study in which the Look is neither unfriendly nor resented. Subject

[1] " The subjectivities remain out of each other's reach, and radically separated."—*L'Etre et le Néant*.

[2] This is part of Sartre's denial of a human *nature*; for him there is only a human *condition*, a phenomenological pattern within which complete freedom obtains. Such freedom, we shall see, is mere indeterminacy. Sartre criticises Proust for presenting the love of Swann for Odette as a *type*—what could Proust, rich bourgeois and homosexual, know about the infinitely varying phenomena comprised under the name " love "? Many of Sartre's analyses read in fact like glosses on Proust—for Proust, after all, began the modern revolt against the florid nineteenth-century concept of character. Nevertheless, Proust has described jealousy as Sartre, with his world of isolated liberties, could never do.

and Object in fact are related as the two sides of a window-tracery, not as the two sides of a coin. Truly enough, in sexual love, the desire to be desired may be paramount; but we suppose there must be a reason why Jean wants to be desired by Jeanne, and not (for instance) by Solange—though the reason may not be easy to discover. The truth is, Sartre's whole analysis is bedevilled by his foible of indeterminate choice; love for him, like will, is a mere fidget. Nevertheless, some persons affect us as interesting and attractive, others—*que voulez-vous?*—do not; even simple beauty is not wholly separable from personality, even lust has its mysterious preferences. If she be not fair for me, what care I how fair she be?

.   .   .   .   .

It is unfortunate that Sartre the philosopher should be known to the general public chiefly by *L'Existentialisme est un Humanisme:* an ill-written pamphlet, rather disingenuous in its argument, and needlessly irritating in its tone. The powerful though perverse mind which produced *L'Etre et le Néant*, the essay on Baudelaire, and the critiques of *Situations* here appears to very poor advantage. So careless is the writing that Sartre can tell us, in the course of a few slim columns, (*a*) that there are two sorts of Existentialists, the Christian and the atheist (he inaccurately classes Jaspers as a Catholic), (*b*) that Existentialism is nothing but the effort to deduce the consequences of a coherent atheist position, and (*c*) that, even if God existed, it would make no matter. (Sartre forgets that, only a few pages back, he has attributed this foolishness—in identical words—to the outmoded " radicalism ".) It is here that he makes the silly remark, much quoted against him by his enemies, " Since I have suppressed God the Father, someone was needed to invent values ". Nevertheless, these impolite and illucid observations are of interest. The attempt to face frankly the consequences of " the death of God "—to find a new " account ' to draw on, now that the capital of the two rationalist centuries is exhausted—that is what Sartrian Existentialism, at its best, is; that is what is valuable in it. Kierkegaard, no doubt, would have been horrified by the phrase " the death of God ", and as Sartre ungracefully admits, there are Christian Existentialists. The old term has sufficient resonance to endure, and to win the allegiance of noble spirits in all ages. But for very many of us today, I fancy, a real and orthodox theist is a little like a Jacobite. We do not, unless we are clergymen, speak of God unquestioningly, as a matter of course; and the clerical fashion of doing so seems to us slightly quaint. And even with Kierkegaard, we saw, God is no longer in the centre. It is not so much His presence we are made to feel, as despair at the failure to reach Him over an infinite gulf; it is less faith than the will-to-faith. In Heidegger we meet with a more unredeemed despair; though we no longer quite know what it is about. But when Sartre speaks of despair, he means at most (it appears in this essay) the bracing feeling of self-reliance[1]; Sartre has really come through despair into an age in which both joy and sorrow have to be re-invented.

What Sartre really cares about—what made his name a sort of inspiration to the war-wracked France of 1945—is not *despair* but *freedom*. The generation depressed by Pétain's weary, and not quite honest, preachment of *Travail, Famille,*

[1] " As for despair, this expression has a very simple meaning. It means that we limit ourselves to counting upon what depends on our own wills, or on the sum of the possibilities which render our action feasible. Say that I am counting on the arrival of a friend, who may be coming by train or by tram. That presupposes that the train will arrive at the scheduled time, or that the tram will not be derailed. I remain in the realm of possibilities . . . for no God and no ' Design ' can adapt the world and its possibilities to my will." Obviously it is absurd to call such discounting of the likelihood of miracles "despair". *L'Etre et le Néant* had spoken of a real despair; but Sartre the politician has really no time for this.

Patrie—caught fire at such phrases as " Man creates himself and his values "; and it did not stop to distinguish too carefully between " idealist " and " realist " senses of the verb *créer*. Do I create the value Truth because the fancy seizes me, or is there in some sense a Truth, which I bring to being, " before " I ever was and " outside of " me?[1] (The whole difficulty, it may be suggested, lies in the ambiguity of those words " before " and " outside of ".) Sartre's language seemed to suggest the former, but at least he would not have said that *L'Etre et le Néant* was a mere flight of fancy. And if moral values are the crux, Sartre certainly upheld freedom in a moral sense, and not merely in an ontological one—just as Heidegger, by implication at least, had praised " authentic living ". Man is " condemned to be free " (surely a true paradox), but he is a *salaud* if he does not realise this situation and make the most of it. For the first time in almost three centuries, the word " freedom " is heard again in metaphysics. We may, I think, find the fact heartening, but we must be careful to determine exactly what Sartre means[2]. He means a number of things; and we shall be sometimes moved to cry out, " Freedom, what sophisms are committed in thy name! "

---

[1] There seems to be a similar confusion in Sartre's theory of the " essence ". On the one hand, a cabbage—unlike a man—has an essence (because it is simply what it is); on the other hand, it receives its essence from my " project " (which differs according as I may wish to eat it, or paint a picture of it, or throw it at a dog).

[2] The novels of Sartre and Simone de Beauvoir read sometimes like caricatures of the " Early Struggles " chapter in a success-story. We are shown people telling each other to be strong who, quite clearly, are incapable of the smallest effort. To parody: " Olga rolled on the floor of the *boîte*, her mouth covered with green foam. Jean was moved by so much purity and plenitude of being. 'Listen', he said. ' I have still 400 francs. With another 400 francs, which I shall steal, we will buy an alarum-clock. That is the first step. *Dare to choose*, and you can easily become a great star of the theatre. *La volonté—c'est tout!* ' " On this side, Existentialism almost merges with " Oxford Groups ".

The whole question of freewill has become almost hopelessly entangled owing to the confusion of two rather distinct ideas; to wit, (*a*) moral freedom (freedom *vis-à-vis* God, or sacrosanct values), and (*b*) psychological freedom (freedom *vis-à-vis* the external world, the genes or whatnot). The first has been often a very anguishing question for believing Christians; the second has little immediate importance for ordinary men, who are inclined to do what they want to do without bothering about what makes them want it. The latter consideration has led pragmatists and positivists to deny that the question has any meaning. Nevertheless the fact that we have seen in our time a religion of " Blood and Soil " shows us that psychological questions can quickly turn to moral ones; and Sartre's flirtations with Marxism should put us on our guard.

Let us very briefly look backward over the history of this fevered problem.

(1) Our pre-Christian ancestors said—for the most part—man is not free, for all things are determined by the Fates, which rule even the Gods. Freedom is either a complete illusion or it is limited to states of mind (" the wise man can be happy on the rack "). Germans like Heidegger really look back to these beginnings; for Heidegger's " authentic living " is nothing else than Stoicism. From this way of feeling we get the Attic Tragedy and (I would say, as its tremendous culmination) the Suffering Messiah. Which leads us " dialectically " to (2).

(2) The medieval Christians said man is free, for he can choose between damnation and (by obeying the rules, and giving up most of his freedom) salvation. Few presumably would willingly choose damnation, though rebels and heresiarchs strangely enough exist, and even abound; but the rules are almost too hard for flesh and blood! However, in that case one can be saved just the same by a repentance. The religion produced moralities rather than tragedies, and,

as moralities have a tendency to be funny, it ended in producing comedy—of the slapstick, buffoonish kind. The
unlucky and outwitted Tempter became at last a " poor
devil ", and from this period (beloved by " amusing "
philosophers) we may date our music-hall—the humble
assertion of man's freedom amidst all troubles. Our M.
Sartre, though no medievalist, combines the romanticism
of the rebel with the more human sympathy for the " poor
devil "; and the combination is well symbolised in the hero
of that curious work, *Saint Genet—Comédien et Martyr.*

(3) The Reformers said, man is not free, for repentance is
" too easy " and leads only to an ignoble commercialism. If a
man is not capable of acting aright, neither will he be
capable of any sincere or worth-while regrets for his failure.
(Some bolder spirits said, why *should* he repent, being denied
the power to go straight?) In fact, man is completely
powerless, unless assisted at every moment by Divine Grace.
It is hard of course on the great majority who, visibly, are
granted no such assistance, and who must accordingly be
damned; but there is no help for it. However, the Reformers
were not much concerned about what is in store for the great
majority, which at the time meant the Papists; and they
themselves (being confident of Grace) became, paradoxically, men of will. This mentality produced a new birth of
Tragedy—the tragedy of questioning and introspection.
The period was indeed tragic, and the result is that most
people today will call themselves anything, almost, sooner
than Protestants, and hate no historical figure so much as
honest Martin Luther. To this, however, there is a notable
exception in the Barthians, who derive largely from the
latter-day Hamlet, Kierkegaard.[1]

[1] In this matter, Kierkegaard's language is nevertheless quite un-
Lutheran. Take the following fine passage: " Omnipotence alone can
take itself back while giving, and this relationship is nothing else but the
independence of the recipient. God's omnipotence is therefore His
goodness. For goodness means to give absolutely, yet in such a way

(4) The eighteenth-century Enlightenment said (in substance) man is free. To the devil with your Sin, Grace and Election, which have given us the most ghastly religious wars, and driven whole regiments of persons out of their wits. Man has his reason which instructs him how to act, and only a fool would be an anti-social being in preference to a social one. If some bits of the old morality are ascetic or irrational, we can do without them. This sympathetic view produced the comedy of manners, to laugh away bigotry and false morality.

(5) The nineteenth century said man is not free. He is conditioned not only in his acts but in his thinking by his environment and heredity (as the materialists said) or by the World-Soul (as the idealists said). Later, a midway school—the Dialectical Materialists—were to say he was conditioned by Economic History. This view—depressing if you will, but not completely intolerable like (3)—produced the nineteenth- and early twentieth-century novel and problem-play.

And that is about where we were when the Existentialists arrived.

We have seen that Existentialists, in various ways, are not far from positions (1), (2) and (3), but have not much to do with (4) and (5). In other words, it is the moral problem that they are chiefly concerned with, and their psychological analyses do not always point in the desired direction. What

that by gradually taking oneself back one makes the recipient independent. From finite power comes only dependence, and omnipotence alone can make something independent, can create something out of nothing which endures of itself, because omnipotence is always taking itself back. Omnipotence is not involved in a relationship to the other, and since there is nothing to which it has any relation, it can give without giving away the very least of its power; it can make the other independent. And that is what is inconceivable: omnipotence can not only bring forth the most imposing of all things, the world in its visible totality, but it can create the most delicate of all things, a creature independent of it."—*Religious Discourses.*

Sartre is rebelling against is what Blake called " Nobodaddy"
the notion of an accusing Eye and Forefinger in the clouds,
or at least of fixed ideals and transcendent values—*les
valeurs-choses*. Moral law is not something eternal and
mysterious, like physical law; it is a set of rules which man
has made, and which man can alter as the circumstances
seem to require it. Orestes says to Zeus in *Les Mouches*:

> Your whole universe is not enough to prove me wrong.
> You are the king of the gods, Jupiter, the king of the stones
> and the stars, the king of the waves of the sea, but you are not
> the king of men.

And by way of contrast to Orestes, we may take the hero
of *L'Enfance d'un Chef*, stepping into a world of idiot ready-
made assumptions as smooth as his pressed trousers,[1] or the
gallery of provincial worthies in *La Nausée*. Man must
assume the entire responsibility for his acts—there is nothing
and nobody that can either condemn or justify him; it is
his grandeur and misery that he is the maker of values. To
pragmatic-minded Anglo-Saxons this will seem like a fuss
about nothing; they have heard it all before. But in the
more scholastic " rationalist " world of the old Continent,
the iconoclast can still make a great stir.

And, of course, Sartre (like Nietzsche, whose language he
repeats) drives this moral relativism beyond all reason. If
there is no pre-existent Good in the structure of things, to
what and for what is man " responsible "? The heroes in
Existentialist plays, like Orestes or the Antigone of Anouïlh,
seem to have no motives for their actions beyond a vague
unrest, and therefore give an impression of unreality. All
their acts are *actes gratuits*. It is true that most of us commit

---

[1] What makes the irony of *L'Enfance d'un Chef* particularly deadly is
that the very games and prayers of the child Lucien—described with a
deceptive sympathy and tenderness—lead insensibly to that preference
for smug illusions which, in the youth, takes forms that are merely
odious. We feel our holiest feelings have been suborned to witness
against us. No satirist except Swift has cut so deep.

gratuitous acts from time to time, inspired by who knows what demon of perversity. Psychologists would call them automatic, and by no means free; but they appeal to us none the less, more than any actions except properly creative ones, by the sense of freedom which they bring. For instance: I have a " date " with a lady, to which I look forward with excitement. For weeks beforehand it fills my thoughts, and such is my impatience that I arrive at the agreed spot a quarter of an hour ahead of time. Suddenly, the strangest fancy seizes me: *I will not keep this appointment.* No one and nothing (I say to myself, with rising anger) shall put this fetter on my movements. Firmly, though it may be with anguish in my heart, I walk away and mingle with the crowd.

Such freaks (of a kind, it may be, with Kierkegaard's " No " to Regine) are perhaps pardonable. But we do not, if we are sane, attempt to conduct the whole of life in this manner; and it is amusing to note the shifts to which Sartre is driven to defend his " total freedom ". Sartre had said that values fly up before us in action, like partridges before a sportsman's gun.[1] His critics replied, " On such a view what

---

[1] One is reminded of this aphorism when one reads Mathieu's reflections in *La Mort dans l'Ame*, as he shoots on the Germans before falling to their bullets: " It was an immense revenge; each shot avenged him for some ancient scruple. A shot for Lola whom I did not dare to rob, a shot for Marcelle whom I ought to have jilted, a shot for Odette whom I did not sleep with. *This* for the books I never dared to write, *this* for the travels I refused myself, *this* for everybody at once whom I wanted to hate and whom I tried to understand. He fired, the commandments went up in smoke—Thou Shalt Love Thy Neighbour as Thyself, bang! into that *gueule de con*, Thou Shalt not Kill, bang! at that dummy opposite. He was firing on Man, on Virtue, on the World—Liberty is Terror. The *Mairie* was ablaze, his head was ablaze—the bullets whistled, free as air. The world will go up in flame, and myself with it. . . . He fired on the handsome officer, on all the beauty of the earth, at the road, at the flowers, at the gardens, on everything he had loved. Beauty ducked obscenely and Mathieu fired again. He fired: he was pure, he was all-powerful, he was free ".

difference is there between the resistant and the Nazi? "
Whereupon Sartre hastened to produce the familiar " Kantian test ", like an ace out of his sleeve (a bit of doctrine
nowhere mentioned by him in *L'Etre et le Néant*). " Thus
our responsibility is much greater than we could have
supposed, for it engages all humanity. . . . In choosing
myself I choose man." But Sartre goes beyond Kant, in
saying not merely that we *should* act as we would prescribe
for all men, but that we *necessarily* do so. " To choose this or
that is to affirm at the same time the value of that which we
choose, for we can never choose the evil; that which we
choose is always the good, and nothing can be good for us
without being good for all." The amalgam of Kant and
Socrates produces an odd effect; but it is obvious that we
are back among " golden rules ", *valeurs-choses* and human
natures, and have forgotten all about the individual. " If
I want to marry, to have children, even if this marriage is
dictated solely by my situation, my passion or my desire, I
thereby engage not only myself but all humanity on the path
of monogamy." Rightly was it said by Gabriel Marcel that
Sartre seems to despise his readers' intelligence. If M. Sartre
is childless, does he condemn us all to childlessness? If King
Solomon had a thousand wives, was he prescribing for all the
Hebrews an equally generous quota? But the brilliant analyses of *L'Etre et le Néant* defy all such clumsy patching. In
that book Sartre had shown, or attempted to show, that the
meaning, like the Day of Judgment, is always ahead of the
act; so that, to put it so, only the last man in the world will
be able to say, such and such acts have proved, on balance,
to have been good—such and such others evil.[1] As Wilde
expressed the same idea in a typical *boutade*:

It is well for our vanity that we slay the criminal, for if we

[1] However, as the last man—like every man—will presumably invent
his values, we may ask why we should trouble ourselves about his verdict.
Sartre a little reminds one of the man who leaves a party early, and

suffered him to live he might show us what we had gained by his crime. It is well for his peace that the saint goes to his martyrdom. He is spared the sight of the horror of his harvest.[1]

In short the Nazi, like Satan in the heresy of Origen, may be saved—proved right—in the end; and many, it already seems, think nothing more urgent than to give him that acquittal. These remarks do not, I think, prove that action may be entirely anarchic; but they do, surely, serve to indicate that it can never be totally free.

For all that, however, there is refreshment in Sartre's theory of " self-choice ". It amounts, properly, not at all to the Kantian rule, but rather to the Shaw-Wilde paradox that we should treat each person and situation as the *exception*. But Sartre has doubled his moral doctrine of liberty with an ontological theory, which goes much farther; and he may not unfairly be charged with " playing on the two tables". According to the latter theory, I choose not only myself—I choose the world; " there are no accidents in a life ". Say that I am a mountain-climber, and come to a precipitous rock. It is not, in the vulgar sense, my " choice " that it shall be unscalable, but its unscalability is relative to and dependent on my choice of climbing; just as, supposing I were a landscape-painter instead of a mountaineer, its dark violet colour would be made effectively real by my project. Again, suppose that I am tortured by political police. I have chosen myself as heroic or weak, and therefore chosen the conditions which bring out these qualities. The torture is a mere *situation* for my project of " squealing " or keeping silence; it is related to my " squealing " (in Gestalt

whose ears burn at the thought of the rattle of tongues in his rear. It will take much to make us believe that Sartre worries about the remote consequences of his acts; few of us do, if we value our sanity. He forgets that, in *L'Etre et le Néant*, he blamed the materialist for such over-conscientiousness: " Everything for him is a consequence, and that is why he is so attentive to the consequences of his acts ".

[1] *The Critic as Artist.*

terms) as a *ground* to a *form*. I am responsible for the war in
which I am involved as much as the Prime Minister who
declared it; for the possibilities of desertion or suicide were
after all open to me. Arguing in this manner, one will be
led to maintain that a half-witted infant in Iceland is
responsible for a rough-house in Peru. Indeed " in a certain
sense, I choose to be born "—in spite of all that Sartre and
Heidegger have told us of *délaissement* and *Geworfenheit*.

So M. Sartre is among the mystics. *A la bonne heure!*
Certainly I do not mean it as a sneer. Every sensitive person
must have felt, at some time, that he has chosen to be born—
that he is responsible for all that happens. Such feelings,
mystical rather than " rational ", are, as I hold, the true
bases of metaphysics, though they are rather novel in French
philosophy—or indeed in the whole classic European tradition. But Sartre has taken over what was most suspect in his
German teachers. Again I must insist that the transcendental Self, which has " chosen to be born ", is never to be
confounded with the empirical Self, which is so largely the
sport of accident—which may attempt to scale cliffs that are
unscalable, which can break down into pitiable insanity
under torture, which even in declaring a war may be
scarcely more responsible than a trigger that is pulled. It is
meaningless, according to Sartre, to say that Racine might
have written another tragedy; the project " Racine " was
completely realised, and would presumably have been
realised if he had died in infancy.[1] Sartre has some right to
claim that his theory is an optimistic one, for it reduces, in

[1] Sartre might well have been instructed here by the analyses of
Leibniz. It is true that if Racine had written more tragedies, instead of
giving himself to religion, he would not be Racine. The Past Condi-
tional is strictly (in the Sartrian terminology) a " magical " tense. But
it does not follow at all that *a person identical with Racine in all other respects*
might not have written more tragedies, or that it is not very easy and
natural to imagine such a person. And this is of course implied by
Sartre's doctrine of free choice.

fact, the very word " tragedy " to meaninglessness. Phèdre, it would follow, also realised her project—which was not to win Hippolite, but to lose both him and life. It is, at least, Hegelianism at its weakest: the doctrine, which we have already glanced at, of the coincidence of Inner and Outer.[1] But it is scarcely reconcilable with the theory of necessary frustration or *échec*. " I must be without remorse or regrets", says Sartre, " as I am without excuse "; and this is true of the super-personal Self, which beholds, in moments of inspired vision, the concatenation of effects and causes. It cannot however be true of the mere mundane Self, which is inserted in the cause-and-effect chain. And if I rule out remorse after my deed, why should I feel " anguish " before it—as in the example given of the commander, on whose part a blunder may cost many lives?[2] The super-personal Self is " without excuse " because it needs no excuse—it is itself the justification of the world; and the mundane Self, lacking that justification (or identification with the Whole), has reason enough to feel " regrets ". The justification of the world is through what Blake called the Imagination, a term always employed by Sartre in the vulgar sense of illusion and evasion;[3] it is the contemplation, not merely of the thinker,

[1] On the phenomenological side, it is the Husserlite doctrine of the identity of the essence with its appearances. But Sartre here forgets his own distinction between essence and existence; the essence Racine did not " exist " until after Racine's death. " The possible ", Sartre has said, " is a structure of the *Pour-Soi*." Perhaps however Sartre means no more than the notion expressed in such vague popular phrases as " Genius always knows what it's doing".

[2] Incidentally, it is this confusion which makes the symbolism of *Les Mouches* very obscure and incoherent. Electra, who gives way to remorse, is delivered from the flies.

[3] This statement, of course, by no means exhausts Sartre's brilliant and subtle analyses. In his first work, *L'Imagination*, he defines the Imaginary as the essence of the cogitative act and " the foundation of the world ", because it is implied in the perpetual " nihilisation ", or transcendence towards the future, which constitutes the real. But

but of the artist—not alone an explanation, but a delighted discovery. And here the Sartrian theory of " choosing the world ", and the other Sartrian theory of transcendence by the *Look*, could, it seems to me, be brought into an interesting relation.

For if Sartre allows a transcendental Self which has *chosen*, why does he stop at the police torture? Why should not this world itself, which in some aspects seems like a torture-chamber, have a meaning that Man in certain moments, can " give " it or " perceive " (for on the transcendental plane the two are one)? But in that case Man is *not* a " useless passion ", who " destroys himself in vain ". Certainly it is well to remember that torture in some part of the world is a daily fact, and possibly will always be so; to say nothing of the torments, less often remembered by Existentialists, visited on the brute creation. Any philosophy which ignores that fact is an academic amusement. But it is not true, as Sartre has said (though one is loath to cavil at words so obviously sincere),[1] that man is most free when he

Sartre is far from an æsthetic conception of total reality, and consequently his æsthetics founder in " æstheticism " on the one hand and " engaged literature " on the other. In *Saint Genet*, Sartre identifies the Imaginary with the Fake, and also with the Evil (which, he now holds, " the Just " have invented)—three conceptions represented for Sartre by the æsthete, the homosexual and the criminal. Genet's dance-hall " queen " Divine—who, when " her " (false) pearl tiara falls off " her " head and is shattered, quickly replaces it with " her " false teeth and continues the dance (crying " *Eh bien, merde, mesdames*, I shall be a queen all the same! ") is, it must be admitted, an apt embodiment of this trinity. If one starts from the complete subjectivity of beauty, and all values, the gesture has its own greatness; and, while one is heartily glad not to have been at the party, one can scarce forbear to cheer.

[1] " We were never more free than during the German occupation. We had lost all our rights, beginning with the right to talk. Every day we were insulted to our faces and had to take it in silence. Under one pretext or another, as workers, Jews or political prisoners, we were deported *en masse*. Everywhere, on billboards, in the newspapers, on the screen, we encountered the revolting and insipid picture of ourselves that our oppressors wanted us to accept. And, because of all this, we

is oppressed, or even when he shows courage under " Third Degree ". The Hunted, as the later history of the Underground movement showed, can very quickly become the Hunters; great endurance is most often found, if we must be realistic, among fanatics and savages. And again, if man has chosen to be born, what makes Sartre declare that " the essences of the relations between consciousnesses is conflict " —a Darwinian doctrine, which is even on anthropological grounds implausible? Has Sartre never had the mystical sense, known to quite ordinary people, not only that " things work together for good ", but that men—even in their seeming conflicts and egoistic projects—collaborate for some cosmic purpose: in short, what to most metaphysicians is axiomatic, that the super-personal Self is *one*? And if that is so, the eye is not only a spy-hole, but can be a window of communication; granted that our perspectives are inescapably distinct (an important truth), they can complement and correct each other. In a sort of harmony we create the moving picture of the world; even if we players are devoured with spleen and jealousy, even if the individual " act " is better than the scenario, we do, in spite of ourselves, work in accord. And as Buber very truly insists, we should regard even " objects " as, to some extent, subjects in their own right, and collaborators as well as " tools ". The eye that " stares ", to be sure, does not so much petrify but rather is petrified—indeed it is already dead; the act of seeing cannot itself be seen and analysed away. As in the legends, Peeping Tom is blinded; Eurydice, the philosopher's Muse, goes back into the Shades.

Sartre might have taken a hint from the fact that a man has *two* eyes; and the fact is largely productive of balance,

were free. . . . The circumstances, atrocious as they often were, finally made it possible for us to live, without pretence or false shame, the hectic and impossible existence that is known as the lot of man."—*La République du Silence.*

not of discord—even though, in a certain sense, the left eye
may not know what the right eye seeth. Each of us is two
persons (*as well as* having an inner Self and an outside); how
can Sartre have ignored a fact so elementary? The Other
Person (indeed, as Dr. Jung has shown, the Other Sex also)[1]
is a mere reflexion, as it were, of that primary duplication—
which is itself a duplication of the original parting of the
elements. And surely any "ontology" should draw the
lines of that great Pattern. We may grant him that the
Pour-Soi "creates" the facets of the *En-Soi*, like a polygon
within a circle; but, by the simple addition of new perspectives, the broken arcs tend to regain the perfect round. And
perhaps it may be not irrational to imagine a finality: a
millennium, not of mere toilers by the hand but of aristocratic sages—contemplators by the eye and the other senses,
who, seeing the total dialectic, will have "rounded it off"
and solved man's problem: a day—exceedingly distant—
when Hegel's vision will be justified, and the weary *Pour-Soi*
can find rest.[2]

Be that as it may, Sartre's liberty really amounts to a complete indeterminacy—a *reductio ad absurdum* of the popular
notion of "doing what one likes". There seems no reason
why I should show courage under torture—just as in the
play *Morts sans Sépulture*, the resistants offer no reason for

---

[1] Simone de Beauvoir, in her massive work *Le Deuxième Sexe*, treats
the female as an artificial fabrication—"an intermediate product
between the eunuch and the male". "The world", laments Mlle. de
Beauvoir, "does not appear to the woman as a 'collection of tools'
situated between her will and its ends, as Heidegger defines it." It is
fortunate that it does not, for that is not a sane way of regarding the
world. However, think what we may of her main thesis—which will
remind older readers of Weininger's once famous paradox—Mlle. de
Beauvoir's treatise abounds in interesting matter, and is written with a
grace and charm which are scarcely Sartre's leading characteristics.
(Some would be so old-fashioned as to call them feminine.)

[2] Elsewhere I have defined the human problem as one of *seeing* the
world in order to *stop* it, and stopping it *by* seeing it.

their heroism. I may wish to create for myself an *être pour autrui* (that is, to win the love of my fellows); but what if my persecutors spread the story that I " squealed "? The only value Sartre recognises is liberty itself—which, thus isolated, does not seem very much of a value. And if one is never so free as in a prison-cell (because never so conscious of one's desire for freedom) it is not obvious *why* any other freedom should be desired. Sartre does not even recognise the Protestant's feeling of " justification ", which is parent to the artist's sense of " inspiration ": the idea that one is free when one is " in truth ", or acting directly from the super-personal Source. And this is strange; for one does not need to insist on his German nurse (and maternal ancestry) to see in him, under the Parisian *allure*, the outlines of the monk of Wittenberg. (Has he not laid the scene of his longest play amidst the German Peasant Wars? Although, again strangely, the Reformation is nowhere mentioned in that play!) Sartrian Existentialism has almost a look of a French Lutheranism—that Lutheranism which has been latent in France for three centuries under the long shadows of Calvin and Descartes. More than this, the Sartrian psychology (derived from Husserl and from the Gestaltists) is a psychology of *patterns*. Perceptions and volitions, it stresses, are conditioned by the wholes of which they are parts; all our choices are contained within a single *choix ultime*. Sartre would doubtless say that the whole man is involved at every moment—like the One Substance of Spinoza embodied entire in each of its modes. But such freedom refers only to the metaphysical pantheistic *essence*, and is equally predic-able of a vegetable or a stone. The truth is that Sartre is struggling (or juggling) with the problem of Freedom— which is the problem of the Irrational—I would almost say, the peculiar problem of the Age of Technics; but the philosopher in him is at perpetual odds with the revolution-ary. (To put it rudely, he is attending to both the cabbage and the goat). It is true that man is free only when he acts "in character", and in character only when he is "in situation", and in situation only when he is "in truth", or in harmony with the wholeness of things; and while in the ontological sense he must doubtless always so act (since he is a part of the Whole), and in the craftsman's sense he so acts when he "creates", in the moral sense he must make a *conscious* choice.[1] In short, essential liberty is not existential liberty. But by dropping the last link in the chain, Sartre has left the others to trail aimlessly on the ground. Thus the situation comes to mean the political situation, the character tends to be identified with the social class, the free act becomes the sporadic violent act—like the surrealist's dream of shooting into a crowd.[2] Freedom becomes the freedom of Descartes' God (hailed by Sartre as a first foreshadowing of Existential Man), whose laws are good simply because He wills them. It was only left for Camus, a moralist but no revolutionist, to preach a morality (fortunately mitigated by pity) of the Absurd.

And yet there is a certain justification for Sartre, which makes his doctrine of freedom, after all, a liberation. It brings to a head the great contemporary revolt (represented in quite opposite ways by Surrealism and Symbolic Logic)

---

[1] For Sartre, choice as such is unreasoned and non-reflective (since he will not allow the term "unconscious")—though it is hard to see how, without reflexion, there can be *angoisse*. The Sartrian hero must not measure the gulf before he leaps. Reflective choice "can only proceed from an error committed in good or bad faith in regard to the ends which I pursue". If I choose to cure myself of stuttering, or of an inferiority complex, my will-to-stutter or to-be-inferior will inevitably take its revenge in some psychopathic form. Only a sudden unreasoned conversion can change the will (a truly Lutheran notion). This has the truth, and the exaggeration, of other current psychological theories; but it seems far-fetched to think that anyone would *choose* (in any fundamental sense) to stutter or to be inferior.

[2] The whole question of "engagement" and "situation" has been far more temperately and sensibly treated by Gabriel Marcel.

against the tyranny of words and concepts; in his essay on Brice Parain and elsewhere, Sartre has insisted on the necessary " checkmate " of language as description of reality. It is a consequence of such failure that man cannot indeed " invent values "—the values are always waiting there round the corner—but he is forced continually to re-invent the names and forms which mediate them. And never has the discrepancy between words and things been wider or more bewildering; for traditional language is hopelessly ill-adapted to the situation of the modern man. The symbol of Plato's Cavern has become reversed: it is the mental abstractions—the " ideals " denounced with Hebraic rage by Lawrence and Chestov—which now oppress us and prevent our seeing. And since poor D. H. died, the ideals have grown teeth and claws. I have spoken of a " wholeness of things" to which man, to be truly free, must be related; but I have been conscious that this must seem like an empty, even a suspect, phrase. The man of today—hemmed in by iron curtains and currency restrictions, scanning the heavens for bombing aeroplanes, believing nothing he hears and hoping for nothing he cannot see—can conceive of no such wholeness; and the rents have become too high for ivory towers. " Wholeness " has come to mean totalitarianism—the deadly peril that lurked even in the great vision of Hegel; or, for the European masses, it has come, not unnaturally, to mean " bourgeois ideology ". Through the litter and rubble of the modern world a man must grope and pick his way by animal instinct; the signposts are torn up and the guide-books out of date.

It is true therefore that the Will today must be a " concrete totality "—something that is felt in the fingers as well as reasoned in the head—something that, while infinitely adaptive and flexible, possesses the force of one's whole being. Nor is this only a fact to be deplored; twentieth-century man's feeling has gained (often under the most fearful stress and tension) a depth-dimension, a spatio-temporal field, which cannot be grasped in any scholastic categories: a truth which we must recognise even in the crudities of the Pragmatists. W. B. Yeats (no lover of the technicists) wrote these excellent words: " Our bodies are nearer to our coherence because nearer to the Unconscious than our thought "—and this, and nothing else, was the doctrine of Lawrence also. Sartre rejects the belief in an " Unconscious ", and he loathes the body with a prurient loathing; yet in spite of an urban background and a scholastic formation, his meaning is not far different. Sartre is the first systematic philosopher to begin, not with the Mind or Matter or the Absolute—but with our human Flesh (for that is all the *être pour autrui* means): the Flesh—its desires, its fears, its sweats and blushes and nauseas, its *frère et cochon* satisfactions. And his dismissal of the Unconscious is, of course, a matter of terms: he has re-baptised it *conscience irréfléchie*, as his *choix original* amounts to the Freudian " complex ". Only, we are struck by one disturbing contrast. Lawrence thought the flesh could be innocent and fine—and why not indeed? Freudians, rightly or wrongly, see the " complex " as a disease. But if Sartre knows of an order of values, however approximative, he has not yet admitted us to the secret.[1] His interest in the technique of

[1] The following words, in the postscript to *L'Etre et le Néant*, have been often quoted against Sartre: " All human activities are equivalent—for all tend to sacrifice man that the Self-Caused may emerge—and all are essentially doomed to failure. Thus it comes to the same thing whether one leads the life of a solitary sot or a leader of peoples". In fairness however the lines which directly follow should also be given: " If one of these existences is to be preferred to the other, it is not because of its real end, but because of the degree of consciousness it possesses of its ideal end; and, in that case, it may happen that the quietism of the solitary drunkard will be more admirable than the vain agitation of the leader". In this there is much truth, and it is perhaps the single bit of wisdom that Sartre has yet uttered on the subject of ethics.

psycho-analysis smacks a little, unfortunately, of his obsession with *voyeurisme* and torture. His proletarianism carries a suggestion of the doctor in *Le Mur*, who mingles with the condemned only to observe their reactions.

Sartre is not, like Malraux or Lawrence of Arabia, a man of action; in spite of his nearness to Pragmatism, he is really far less interested in " technics " even than Heidegger. He is a little professor who has been rudely flung upon the human reality, and is never tired of telling us all about it. He finds the World, the Flesh and the Devil very much more interesting than the True, the Good and the Beautiful; and, while we shake our wise heads, we can surely feel a certain rush of sympathy. But at first, in *La Nausée* (a work which, with all its fierce satire, has much tenderness and beauty), his reaction was bewilderment, and a seeking in odd places for an æsthetic absolution. Roquentin, as he leaves the park, turns back to the offending vegetation in a puzzled, more humble, mood:

The smile of the trees, of the clump of laurels, it all *wanted to say something*; that was the true secret of existence. I remembered that one Sunday, not more than three weeks ago, I had already noticed in things a sort of look of complicity. Was it to me that it was addressed? I felt with exasperation that I had no means of discovering. No means. Nevertheless it was there, in the expectancy, it resembled a look. It was there, in the trunk of the chestnut-tree . . . it was *the* chestnut-tree. The things—one would almost have said thoughts which stopped half-way, which got lost, which forgot what they had wanted to say and remained like that, swaying, with a queer little meaning which defeated them. It irritated me, this little meaning: I *couldn't* understand it, even if I should remain seven centuries leaning against the railings; I had learnt everything I could know about existence. I went off, I returned to the hotel, and as you see, I wrote.

This goes deeper, certainly, than much that Sartre has

written on the *Look*. And listening to a trivial rag-time song on the gramophone of a *bistro*, he reflects:

Behind the existent which drips from moment to moment, without past, without future, behind these sounds which dissolve from day to day, flake off and slide into extinction, the melody remains the same, young and strong, like a relentless witness.

This is not the tedious Sartre of *le projet*. And—how has it not been noticed?—he puts the whole of his later doctrine, mockingly, into the mouth of the foolish " *autodidacte* ". The latter is epitomising the gospel of some American prophet:

" He concluded ", said the Autodidacte in a consoling tone, " in favour of a determined optimism. Life has a meaning if one wishes to give it a meaning. One must first of all act, throw oneself into an enterprise. If one goes on to reflect, the die is cast, one is *engaged*. I don't know what you think about it, monsieur? "
" Nothing ", I said.
Or rather I think it is precisely the sort of lie which the commercial traveller, the two young people and the old white-haired gent [other personages present] are always telling themselves.

About this time, however, the historical dialectic developed an excess of animation. Hitler dawned over Europe, like Western Man's obscene *Alter Ego* in a surrealist apocalypse;[1]

---

[1] Sartre is so lacking in a sense for history that, in his admirable dissection of anti-Semitism, he has missed the main point—which is a little surprising, for it is an Existentialist point. Though the Catholic Church sensibly condemns racialism, anti-Semitism is nevertheless the " shadow-side " of historic Christianity, and cannot ever really be exorcised from it. The orthodox Christian must believe in *les valeurs-choses*—substances, incarnate Absolutes. Anti-Semitism is the necessary symptom of the European's *mauvaise foi*—his torturing position of despising the Synagogue while worshipping a Jew. Placing his good and evil outside of him, he must cling to a medieval melodramatisation to hold them apart—no Betrayal, no Redemption: otherwise his two Absolutes would be in danger of collapsing, and he would feel himself in a *Néant*.

after the pitiable *Sursis* came the *Sabbat* of the Defeat, the Occupation—the *Führer* trotted up the Eiffel Tower, the torture-squads were released on France. Sartre, the slippered novelist-professor (whose interest in politics had till then been of the slightest) was confronted, like all his countrymen, with a very anguishing *choice*; the dreary business-man's slogan of *Action* for a moment became honourable and almost epical. By the choice he made and his deciding for Action, he saved the credit of French intellect; and he evolved, out of his Husserl and his Heidegger, a philosophy appropriate to the time—a queer stoical doctrine of the Will against the World, burrowing like a mole without faith or hope. For in that night, lit only by the isolated raids of the " Underground ", nothing any more made sense— except a few men's honour and courage to the death.

The thinker and satirist became, of necessity, a leader; and perhaps it might have been better for him had he died then, though we would have lost some entertaining works— seeing that in the present " post-war " he seems not to have a notion what to be at. The tentative Platonic musings of *La Nausée* are long forgotten; and the austere dogmas of *L'Etre et le Néant*, in times of peace and comparative normality, no longer fit. Sartre, who has rejected the Christians, is in turn rejected by the Marxists; for his doctrine of the solitary Will, suitable enough for guerrilla-fighters, can today mean only " Trotskyism " and the Permanent Revolution. I said to a Frenchman that Sartre could yet be a force in the world. " You are wrong", he replied, " Sartre is alone, and has been alone for the past eight years—apart from a committee of five or six people whose lives extend in other directions than Sartre's. But the ' force ' (not a ' force in the world ') is undeniable—unrelenting and undamped by any number of wet blankets." In such a predicament stoicism turns to pose, the cult of the Will becomes sterile and, in effect, evil. Sartre, who might have been a martyr, becomes a comedian; another step, and he will be (what he is not) a charlatan. He ends by embracing the diabolist paradox, which he criticised in Baudelaire, that evil is a voluntary martyrdom. The outcasts' champion exchanges the " Underground " for the " Underworld ". He can find no one left to praise except the criminal.[1]

Existentialists have a notable difficulty in finishing their books: of necessity, for their philosophy—staying close to the movement of life—can have no finality.[2] Heidegger will never finish *Sein und Zeit*, Sartre will never conclude his distressing chronicle-novel—he died, we feel, essentially, when he " killed off " its hero. At the close of *L'Etre et le*

[1] In *Qu'est-ce que la Littérature?* Sartre gives us an artistic application of his doctrine, which he relates to the possibility of a new proletarian literature. " After Saint-Exupéry, after Hemingway, how could we dream of merely describing? We must plunge things into Action. Their density of being will be measured for the reader by the multiplicity of practical relations which they maintain with the character. Have the mountain climbed by the smuggler, the customs officer and the guerill-ero, have it flown over by the aviator, and the mountain will suddenly surge from these connected actions and jump out of your book like a jack-in-the-box." This is excellent—though smugglers and customs officers are seldom literary artists. But Sartre can always be trusted to give the *reductio ad absurdum*. In *Saint Genet* he writes: " Genet is taken with raging desires to violate the indifference of being, to act, and— since he is forbidden to do it in the more usual ways—let it be by pillage. He will learn the density of being by the effort which it costs him to destroy it. He will rob, smash, lay waste, *to put out all these eyes which stare at him*. [My italics.] Theft is not only a method of living: it is a sacred destruction. In a burglary, one must tear away the bars, wrench doors from their hinges, kill the dogs, lull the suspicions of the watchmen. If all goes well, one *enters into a man. . . ."* The imagery which follows would need to be rendered into Latin.

[2] This consideration has prevented Gabriel Marcel (an extremely fine thinker) from ever attempting to construct a system. It has not however prevented him accepting the Catholic system, in which some of his earlier insights cannot with strictness be contained. Other admirable but over-nebulous minds have accommodated themselves within Marxism. That is the danger of too great a distrust of concep-tual thought. In the words of Blake: "I must create a system myself or be enslaved by another man's."

Néant he posed some queries (apt to be overlooked by his exhausted readers), such as these: " Is it possible that liberty, as the source of value, should take itself for value, or must it necessarily define itself in relation to a transcendental value which haunts it? " " Will liberty, in taking itself for an end, escape from all *situation*? " He left these questions open, though it is generally assumed he closed them; but he promised to deal with them in another work. That work has never appeared; there are some things, after all, that are beyond a Sartre. When our Moses returned a second time from the heights, he brought with him no Tables of the Law, but—a work worthy in bulk to be put beside its predecessor—the scatological apotheosis of Genet!

" Man ", said Berdyaev (borrowing a doctrine from Boehme), " is the child of God and the child of freedom—of nothing, of non-being, *to mēon*." Eros, in Plato's myth, was the child of Plenty and of Want. Freedom unattached to Value—Want without an object—is in fact the definition of Evil. And it seems that Sartre has realised it, but without misgivings. In *Genet*, the *En-Soi* and *Pour-Soi* have changed their names—they now appear as *le Bien* and *le Mal;* but the second is still, on the whole, the hero. " The being of Evil is at once the Being of Not-Being and the Not-Being of Being ". This, we have seen, was in the earlier work the definition of Man. Such an assimilation is an insane extreme of logic—that over-exaltation of the abstract which France, in Jansenism and Jacobinism, has given to the world; Man, however, is also a synthesis (also the " concrete universal ") or, in Berdyaev's language, a child of God. Sartre has tried to look into the very bottom of Pascal's chasm; and, as Nietzsche warned, the Abyss has looked into him. For if man is existence and not essence, then he is not " problematic " but (as Marcel says) " mysterious "; and to attempt to define him is to define the Mass-Man only, or, what is in reality the same, the anti-social individual. Sartre, with his superb

intellectual vitality, is also, after all, of the " lost generation ": the generation which destroyed itself that Nothing
might be born.

. . . . .

And yet finally, I get little impression of evil in Sartre,
but rather of a great courage and a great gaiety—alas, that
these things should be not enough. He is one of those people
of whom solemn persons say, just because they are amusing,
" Do you think he can be sincere? " He can make the ideas
dance to his piping, and he has let loose the Mænads in the
academic grove; we should not grumble overmuch, at so
lavish a feast of reason, if unreason has also its place. There
is a fool in Sartre who, in a less logical climate and a less
austere time, would be a happy fool; being a Frenchman
who (in more than the usual sense) *a vu le loup*, he wears a
red cap and builds a guillotine for " Values ". Even in
his grittiest chapters (and my stomach in these matters is as an
old maid's), the general effect is one of mental exhilaration.
He has given back to literature a density, a frame of reference, which it lacked between the two wars; he has restored
to things their outside and their skin, even if it was with
loathing—and the loathing was partly at least ironical. He
is a fighter who can lay about him from sheer lustiness, without counting on whose heads the blows may fall; no Totali-
taria, certainly, will ever regiment him—no capitalist will
buy him. He may have no statue at any time on this earth—
even in France, that land of statues; and he would make a
strange figure enough in any Heaven. But though the
inhabitants of the place will crowd to hear him, he will be
alone, I think, even in Hell.

CONCLUSION

SYNOPSIS

Our trio have led us to the frontiers of a philosophy we can repose in— a philosophy of direct poetic apprehension; but they cannot enter that Promised Land, for they know little of the non-rational but its Dread. Their religious followers or critics speak (as Kierkegaard often spoke, and spoke finely) the old phrases of Christian love; but Love has become a rationalised and utilitarian emotion, tending to the abolition of " excellent differences ". Social love has come to be the denier of a man's " own truth ", proclaimed in the sphere of conscience by Luther and in that of intellect by Descartes. The over-emphasis of Love (in the modern riot of ideals and community values) has logically produced Hate; whereas the acceptance of sharp oppositions may lead to sensitive adjustment. Such are the oppositions between Self and Other (Sartre), Life and Death (Heidegger), the Human and the Divine (Kierkegaard). They are in essence the same opposition, and, as mystics have said, ultimately illusory; but they can only be transcended by those who have felt them in their full force, while remaining true to their humanity, their selfhood, and to life itself.

WE have completed our voyage: a Dantesque journey *à rebours* through the heavens of Kierkegaard, Heidegger's purgatorial experience of the tomb, and finally the sad inferno of Sartre. It remains for other philosophers to come through and possess the Earth—the material æsthetic Fact, stranger than any super-earthly fiction. Behind all of our three thinkers stands the mighty figure of Hegel, who first attempted that great task—though

147

in terms of a verbal dialectic which we today find forced and arbitrary. There have been many revolts against that Master, but the Existentialists alone, while vigorously rebelling, are in the Succession. Nevertheless it is true that none of them—in spite of the claims of their many fervent disciples—has given us a new world-view that we can accept. They are very sound in showing that Grand Systems are no longer possible; for the ambiguities of existence are too dense to be dissected out by any logical knife. But they are wrong in so far as they attempt, inconsistently, to build systems of their own—exchanging, so to say, the dissecting-knife for the psychological (or phenomenological) X-rays. It is evident that we cannot live with the Existentialist universe: for it omits all of our non-rational intuitions except the single one of Dread. It undervalues what Sartre calls the " Imaginary " and the " Magical " (the natures and virtues and mysterious inter-relations of Things, and of Persons in so far as Persons are also Things), the non-logical knowledge of women, children and animals, and finally almost all tradition. In this it commits the modern fault which Lord Russell (himself a bad offender in this respect) has called " cosmic impiety ". Nevertheless these writers also are poets, and their analyses, like some pictures of the Surrealists, are in part an approach to Nature through her strangeness. (Sartre's discussion of the " psychology " of substances is of especial interest.) Existentialism is a phase of the revolt against an over-intellectualist tradition—a tradition from which it has not yet worked itself free.[1] That revolt began during the late eighteenth-century Enlightenment as a " Romantic Agony ", or nostalgia for

[1] One reason for the strangeness of the Existentialists' writing is their sparing use of such words as " relatively ", " potentially " and "unconsciously ". In their world, there are no continuities or gradual transitions—all is shock and counter-shock. Every creation is from the Void, every god is from the machine. In the end, this philosophy of the concrete is apt to seem more abstract and artificial than any system of the past.

the Dark; though one can trace it, if one wishes, through the Renaissance and the Middle Ages in the Secret Cults. Existentialism is its last chapter—opened by the queer Byronic pietist Kierkegaard, the man who broke an engagement because he felt himself " engaged ".

Against Heidegger and Sartre, the religious wing of Existentialism—Marcel, Buber, Jaspers—asserts the mystery and dignity of love, the truth that man is most truly human in community, the synthesis of the *I and Thou*. They are quite clearly right; they are safer guides than their opponents. One feels, however, that they have missed the Journey through Dread, or rather (to speak more accurately) they do not help us to experience it—the moment so powerfully conveyed even by the Christian Kierkegaard in which *all* helpers fail and comforts flee. When their exaggerations have been discounted, there remains real nourishment in Kierkegaard's sense of a cosmic guilt, in Heidegger's shock of solitude before Death, in Sartre's stress on the Challenge of the minute-to-minute and the unprompted Choice. We have said in answer to Sartre that the Transcendental is *one* —a Unity which gives all particulars their meaning. That is no more than all the greatest have held; but if, theoretically, it is the first truth of philosophy, in the practical order it is (for a modern consciousness at least) the very last. It can be reached only by men and women who have learnt, in the proud phrase, *their own truth*—who are able to say like Luther, " Here I stand, I cannot do otherwise "—who have discovered, in a word, what W. B. Yeats called " the awful virginity of the soul ". The blessedness of love—a vitalising doctrine to the first Christians—has degenerated into the absolutism of the average, the apotheosis of the common, the now dismally familiar condition of " Everyone everyone-else's keeper "; and, in totalitarian states, into something viler still. The One of mystics has turned into the very mundane *one* (*das Man*) of Heidegger. The word

" love ", similarly to the word " God ", bears the load of centuries of rationalisation; by the logic of objectified concepts, love has become a generator of its opposite—hate. Its fevers must be allayed in the *Néant* of an older, more unconscious world-feeling; if we have less of the Mob's " community-mindedness "[1] we shall have less of the Mob's cruelty also. The *Other*, in his sheer difference, must be recognised and respected as terrible, before he is accepted as lovable. He must be seen as Blake's Tiger—even in his virtues—before he can be Blake's Lamb.

But the issue is not only a social, but also a philosophical one—not only " affective " but " cognitive ". Those who call us back to traditional truisms (which still are true, but in danger of debasement) would lose all that we have learnt by the Idealist experience: the discovery that the world exists for, and in relation to, the Mind. Every philosophy, after Descartes, must start from the abyss of Doubt—doubt not merely of God but of a Cosmos. It must be an adventure of re-creation and reconquest. That reconquest, with Descartes, was a compromise—with Kant, it was a treaty of demarcation—with Hegel, it was an illusion of empire; all these great captains finally have failed. The world is still there, outside us, for the winning. The artist, in my belief, must be called in aid where the doctors admit defeat. The gramophone record in the low *bistro* still whispers to us of a *drôle de petit sens*, while the churches and the lecture-rooms give us back only a " dusty answer ".

Both thought and love must aim beyond themselves. The lover must surpass, not only himself, but love. If I love the

---

[1] I do not of course mean to associate the distinguished thinkers I have mentioned with such vulgarism; indeed they have denounced the urban abjection far more, and more wisely, than have Heidegger and Sartre, who hail the age of technology. I mean only that the emphasis on *social* values has produced the modern malady, and is not the best means of curing it. These philosophers all start with the *I*; only, in my opinion at least, they reach the *Thou* too easily.

Other because he is my " brother ", a child of God, this is still only an extension of myself; I am keeping love, so to speak, in the family. I must love him (if the term can still be used) like a non-human object, like the trees in the park or the gramophone disc—even if it be with nausea: drawn by his *sorte d'air complice*, his *drôle de petit sens*. For " I am not what I am and I am what I am not "; and it is my fate— tragic, comic, sad or joyful as you choose to regard it—to seek the Oneness of opposites in which is peace. (It is tragic because peace, like death, can never be enjoyed as a positive state; it is joyful because, when I look at the total effort of Time and World, I can see a pattern which is One.) And again, the thinker must aim beyond " dialectic "—or con- fess that the dialectic (though it is there) is beyond him. If I *think* the Other, because he is implied negatively in the affirmation of myself, I leave out nearly everything about him. Existence, as Kant expressed it, is not a predicate. And if I should continue the process so far as to encompass the whole world (though a superhuman intelligence might accomplish it) I would still be only grinding out words. Such " thought " is a mere framework—valueless unless it be filled in by direct æsthetic apprehension. Hegel spoke of a " concrete universal ", but who ever felt his universe as concrete? In the excellent phrase of Kierkegaard, that cloud-palace was not meant for living in.

The popular reaction to Hegel was partly right, but not wholly so; for there *is* an Idea (of which Time is the working- out) as there is a Law of Gravity. Only, it is hidden by the exteriority of things—like the solid-seeming crust of the earth, almost unnoticed by the professor on his happy rounds. But in volcanic epochs that " Outside " does strange things, and is encountered with dread and loathing; the world—once a pretty picture to hang on the study wall— jumps out at you, in Sartre's phrase, like a jack-in-the-box. Dürer's Knight has returned, as the lonely " displaced " fatalist—and his companions are still Death and the Devil. The Other is no longer my mere logical negative, nor is he just my " fellow-man ", as the left hand is the fellow of the right. He is, like myself, *alone*—and it is on that plane of Aloneness, with all its discomfort and shock, that I must meet him. The Other is the only limit to my infinite Aloneness, out of which mere reason (and even brotherly love) can never break. We can put together our three Masters and say that the Other is my death, that Death is in the end the only Other, but that it has an Other Face which is the One, or, if you wish it, God.

That Other Face we can never see, for it is turned away from us and turns as we turn—it is indeed our very Self; but the attempt to gain sight of it causes all the agitation which is life. It cannot well be described in philosophic prose; and those who decry or scoff at it are often nearer to it than its zealous seekers. Beauty today is not a word for poets but for beauty specialists; but most men know what it is that seems always to flee, and will not be held captive even by a word. It can make thé Outside of things transparent, and even fuse (as talk of " Love " for us today cannot) the Me and Thee.[1] If our three subjects throw long shadows, it is because, I believe, the light of a new eɪa of the world is close to them. The " Outside "—the barrier-wall between Self and Self—is indeed, as the Indian sages say, illusion; for to think of an " Inner " and an " Outer " is to think spatially, as Kant did with his Things-in-themselves and Ideas-in-the-Mind. (And Heidegger, and still more Sartre, are by no means free from the same Kantian error.) But to proclaim the illusoriness of Matter does not, perhaps, much advance us at the present time; the scientists, after all, affirm no less,

---

[1] The " I and Thou " sect bring to one's mind (with apologies to that fine spirit, Martin Buber) the well-known lines of Fitzgerald:

" Some little talk awhile of Me and Thee
There was—and then no more of Thee and Me."

and such loftiness leads us back into the easy mazes of Idealism. We need today, not to deny the material world, but to *look at* it—freed from abstractions and names; like the survivor of a shipwreck, contemplating his store of fragments. When the Zarathustra of Nietzsche went searching for the " Higher Man ", he encountered among others on his way the " Ugliest Man ", whom he called the Murderer of God—for God Himself could not look on the immensity of his ugliness and live. (Or—what is really the same thing— such ugliness could not endure the All-Seeing Eye. " *J'ai supprimé Dieu le Père. . . .*") That Ugliness is the shudder of the Flesh—the shudder of a man naked, solitary and bewildered, before his last and widest ditch. It is what we are coming to call the " existential " experience—the peculiar experience of our time, though present of course in all times. But the shudder before the paradox of Fate and Will (variously stated by our three philosophers) can turn to the glow of poetic apprehension, or the " essential " experience. Here our guide, I think, will not be any one of the rationalists of the old Continent, but English Lawrence—that true poet-thinker who yet (in Nietzsche's phrase) remained faithful to the Earth. In the perhaps too hopeful " farewell " of Sartre's great Summa, *Nous y consacrerons un prochain ouvrage.*

APPENDIX

A NOTE ON THE DIALECTIC

STRANGELY, no Hegelian seems to have noted that the *Antithesis* in the formula, being the very principle of contradiction, is at once divisible into 1st and 2nd Antithesis—as the *Synthesis* is in fact a 2nd *Thesis*. It is this hidden *2nd Antithesis* that is forever turning the logic into a baffling three-card trick. We may, however, distinguish four primary forms of the dialectic, corresponding to the four dialectical positions, as follows:

1st Figure (*The Figure of Logic*)

A		Zero
	B	Minus
		C	Plus
A		Unity
	B	Duality
		C	Trinity

This is the dialectic of pure mathematical ideas or *essences*—the impure 2nd Antithesis of contingency or *existence* cannot rise into this Olympus. (The number 4 by division and subdivision returns to the unity, and so on.) It was by attempting to apply this merely logical formula to the material world that Hegel fell into confusion. In the order of Being, the Nothing becomes a Something by self-limitation; in the order of Thought, the Unity becomes a Trinity by self-division. The Hegelian Being-which-is-Not-Being is the Zero; the Not-Being which negates it is the Minus; their synthesis, Becoming, is the Plus—a first position.

In the 2nd Figure the great Break first appears—in the centre. We have now come out of the Eden of pure Ideas, and we see how the Plant inverts itself and becomes the Man. The *fruit* (the primary synthesis) is detached from the ancestral tree of

155

2nd Figure (The Figure of Nature)

A			Root	East	Air
	B		Flower	South	Fire
		C	Fruit	West	Water
	D		Seed: Womb	North: Winter	Earth: Mineral
A			Heart	Spring	Vegetable
	B		Loins	Summer	Animal
		C	Head	Autumn	Human

unconscious nature by force of the Magnetic North of sex and outward environment—to become in turn the human person's sensitive *heart*, his *head* like a reversed *root* groping its way heavenward (i.e. to the position of pure contemplation). The formless liquidity, by its own inherent weight—as of the fall of a hammer—splits into the solid particles of Earth: out of which Life arises, like the raising again of the hammer (the fourth " element " and the first " kingdom " being, of course, the same—the matrix of *Matter*, or Seed of the cosmic Tree). The hardening of the Earth corresponds to the Crucifixion of the natural (i.e. reasonable or " reflective ") man at the supreme Break in our history, when the world made the great Reversal, seeking its way back to Eden.

3rd Figure (The Figure of Man)

A			Child	Sensation
	B		Youth	Perception
		C	Maid	Cognition
	D		Man	Volition
		C	Wife	Action
	D		Mother	Intuition
A			Whole-Man	Contemplation

This is the interweaving spiral of the sexes; it might be called the figure of counterpoint—and comedy. There are now *two* Breaks, because there are two sexes—the Break in the life of the male is the affirmation of the *will* in embracing marriage, in the life of the female it is the *intuition* of her *destiny* in the realisation of maternity. The condition of permanence gives the initiative to the female, because permanence (the cognitive) is the mode of femaleness—

looking to the Past—as change (the perceptive) is that of maleness—looking to the Future; the object of the reversal, however, is that the female may give back to the male (purged of the illusions of infinite choice) the freedom he has surrendered, the fresh initiative whose symbol is the new child, a spontaneity of feeling detached from mere outward perception—the quick of the Present.

4th Figure (*The Figure of the World*)

A		Egyptian	Causality	Point
	B	Mycenean	Time	Line
	D	Classical	Space	Plane
	C	Byzantine	Matter	Solid: Centre
	B	Medieval	Life	Radius
	D	Modern	Death	Circumference
A			Mind	Sphere

This might be called the figure of tragedy—so to say, the bass in the concerto. Here, each half of the movement breaks in the centre—every great culture is disrupted by the internal stresses which it generates. It is indeed significant that the Christian Church should have been first divided, in the eleventh century, over this very point: for the insertion of the *Filioque* clause in the Creed—which in effect quadrupled the Trinity—stands as the earliest recognition of that *2nd Antithesis*, or irrational dæmonic force, under whose sign our age groans and travails. As the tension of the ancient world was the outer, primordial strife between Time and Space, so the tension of the Christian world is the inner one between Life and Death; and as the first resulted in the abstract universal of the Idea—or contingent oneness—so the second is labouring in turn to produce the concrete universal, the Individual—the realisation of personality as self-moved and self-caused oneness.

Farther than this I should not attempt—even if it were the place—to go. I wish merely to suggest that there *is* a dialectic, but that we cannot follow it very far, owing to the complexity of the real and the ambiguity of words—in short, that spirit of irreducible contradiction and frustration which I have called the 2nd Antithesis, and whose votaries are the Existentialists. Even the above paradigms will be disputed, with good right: for others will understand different things (in many cases) by the same words, and see the correspondences differently. The 4th Figure, which is especially the figure of the 2nd Antithesis, is of course particularly elusive and treacherous; hence the certain defeat of all over-schematic philosophies of history. But if any Hegelian should pronounce my four figures to be foolishness, let him try to apply his dialectic to the seasons—the simplest of the great frameworks within which we live.

INDEX